Praise for *Public Sector M...*

'Joanne Sweeney's newly updated *Public Sector Marketing Pro* has everything you need to know about digital marketing and social media in one easy-to-read guide. Her insightful advice will help you transform your marketing communications work. A game changer!'

MARILYN WILKES, director, communications,
MacMillan Center, Yale University

'I wouldn't be without the book. Joanne Sweeney speaks in such an informed way about the value of marketing in the public sector. Her expertise and enthusiasm for working together to build a network of professionals are infectious and inspiring!'

SHEILA BYRNES, communications manager, Marine Institute

'Joanne Sweeney is a Digital Ninja Queen! This book arms you with the tools you need to lead digital marketing and transformation. You'll learn the communication and change management techniques to support an agile and future-focused approach to your business strategy—and how to implement them. A must-read for all leaders in public sector to support our delivery in an ever-changing environment.'

MARIA McCANN, organisational psychologist;
assistant national director, digital organisational change, HSE

'Too often public agencies have the communications mindset of "Here's what you need to know." Joanne Sweeney raises the bar with an easy-to-follow system to reassess social media to manage the message in a medium of chaos and misinformation.'

ERIC JAY TOLL, communications manager, City of Phoenix

'The "how to" social media guide for public agencies to better reach the citizens they serve. From seeking assistance for investigations to communicating about incidents and events to marketing programmes and projects, the widespread use of social media channels is essential. Every public safety agency should have this book.'

DR STEPHEN A. MORREALE, professor, criminal justice, Worcester State University; special agent (retd), DEA

'Joanne Sweeney makes complex digital marketing strategies and ideas seem achievable and exciting. Couple this with how she proved her agility both during and after a global pandemic as a communications leader herself, and you're in for a real treat!'

CHRIS DUCKER, bestselling author, *Rise of the Youpreneur*

'Drawing on first-hand research and experience gathered throughout a two-decade career in media and communications, Joanne Sweeney's revised book oozes with her enthusiasm for digital communications and identifies key elements that will allow you to develop and optimise your social strategies.'

ALISON MALONEY, digital media and communications specialist, Teagasc

'Insightful and well researched, Joanne Sweeney's *Public Sector Marketing Pro* is a must-read for anyone planning or delivering marketing within the public sector, regardless of their experience level!'

LINZI JONES, copywriter, The Jones Edit

'An essential read for public sector marketing pros and government communicators. This book will help guide us as we come out of the pandemic with its "how to" guides, chapter-by-chapter checklists and clear and practical advice.'

MUIRIOSA RYAN, social media manager, HSE

'The perfect resource to keep on your desk and refer to as you work through marketing and communications projects. Packed full of sound, usable advice and tips that are relevant in any industry.'

DAVID CORSCADDEN, digital engagement and
communications officer, Irish Universities Association

'The comprehensive bible public sector professionals need in a post-pandemic world to navigate the fast-changing landscape of digital media, marketing and communications. Expert Joanne Sweeney teaches you every scenario from agile planning to crisis management. Don't leave your home office without it.'

NIAMH CONNOLLY, marketing and communications manager,
College of Medicine, Nursing & Health Sciences, NUI Galway

'Joanne Sweeney's updated book is perfect for the blink-and-you-miss-it pace of digital comms. Her snappy, succinct style reveals her audience-savvy broadcast journo background and heart for digital transformation serving the public interest by cutting quickly to the heart of what matters, what works and, more importantly, what's coming.'

LISA LEILANI WILLIAMS, public affairs advisor,
Pacific Islands Forum Secretariat

'Joanne Sweeney speaks plainly about the responsibility the public sector has to provide citizens with accurate, honest, transparent and up-to-date information on their terms—and what they need to do to stay ahead.'

BOBBY BARBOUR, MABS marketing and communications manager,
Citizens Information Board

'*Public Sector Marketing Pro* should be top of your reading list if you are working in public sector marketing. It is specifically written to support the unique work we do.'

YVONNE MORRISSEY, communications manager,
HSE National Immunisation Office

'Joanne Sweeney has shared her knowledge and expertise in digital marketing for the public sector and provides practical tips, insights and toolkits which give you the confidence to jump into the digital arena.'

HELENA MURPHY, social media lead, communications, eHealth & Disruptive Technologies, HSE

'A pleasure to read and easy to digest. Joanne Sweeney's no-nonsense, clear and concise style makes this book the go-to manual for organisations serious about upping their game.'

DR GRAINNE KETELAAR, lecturer, ATU

'Digital transformation becomes straightforward with Joanne Sweeney's knowledge and practical advice. Essential reading.'

CATHERINE COSTELLO, librarian, Wicklow County Council

'From Joanne Sweeney's blueprint for designing a tailored social media campaign, to her section on crisis management in the Digital Age, she has once again produced a must-read for anyone looking to fully utilise the potential of social media.'

EDDIE GOLDEN, superintendent, An Garda Síochána

Public Sector Marketing Pro

REVISED FOR A POST-PANDEMIC WORLD

Public Sector
Marketing Pro

The Definitive Guide to Digital
Marketing and Social Media for
Government and Public Sector

JOANNE SWEENEY

FOREWORD BY TOM COCHRAN
chief digital advisor, White House, under President Obama

JS PRESS

ISBN 978-1-9161149-2-0 (paperback)
ISBN 978-1-9161149-3-7 (ebook)

JS Press
publicsectormarketingpros.com

Produced by Page Two
pagetwo.com

Edited by Amanda Lewis and Emily Schultz
Copyedited by Melissa Edwards
Proofread by Alison Strobel
Cover and interior design by Taysia Louie
Interior illustrations by Michelle Clement,
Taysia Louie and Djameela Daniels
Author photo by Michelle Dolan,
Wonky Eye Photography, Galway, Ireland

publicsectormarketingpros.com

THIS BOOK IS DEDICATED to the millions of frontline workers who showed up while we stayed home, who put themselves at risk while we came out when it was deemed safe.

This book is also dedicated to the '*heroes that do the silent work,*' an iconic statement from Dr Mike Ryan, executive director of the Emergencies Programme at the World Health Organization, that caught my attention in the early days of COVID-19.

To media and social media professionals working in public sector and government, thank you. You too have played a significant role in saving lives and empowering citizens.

To my lockdown buddies, my children, Sophie (27) and Bobby (13), it really was a special time for us as a family. May we live out the best lessons taught to us in living through a pandemic.

About the Author

JOANNE SWEENEY IS founder of the Digital Training Institute and a passionate writer, podcaster and vlogger. A former broadcast journalist, Joanne has an impressive 21-year career in all forms of media and communications, from PR to lecturing, corporate communications, digital marketing and social media. She is the founder of Public Sector Marketing Institute, a specialist digital communications agency for government and public sector organisations.

Joanne is the host of the *Public Sector Marketing Show Podcast* and organiser of the Public Sector Digital Marketing Summit. Her first book, *Social Media Under Investigation: Law Enforcement and the Social Web*, takes a forensic look at how police forces are leveraging social media for crime investigation, public relations and community engagement. She has also developed a suite of accredited online courses and coaching programmes to help public sector marketing pros excel in digital communications. Her global audience of clients come from sectors such as politics, national and local government, higher education, policing, science, defence, diplomacy and consumer affairs.

A life-long learner, Joanne holds 11 academic and professional qualifications, including a master's degree in journalism and a master's degree in digital marketing. Joanne is an advanced digital marketing trainer for Google and is a regular on the speaker circuit and has appeared on numerous stages in the US, Australia, mainland Europe, the UK and Ireland. She was a speaker at Meta's first Government Digital Transformation Summit in 2021.

Acknowledgements

THIS BOOK HAS been a passion project for me, and it has been in my head for many years. However, to finally publish it required input and inspiration from a number of people who deserve acknowledgement.

First, I must acknowledge the most special people in my life who do not have my time or attention when I am writing, although they appreciate hugely my intentions and respect my labours of love and work. To my children, Sophie (27) and Bobby (13), who are a constant source of support and inspiration for me and for whom I work so damn hard. Thank you. Your unconditional love provides me with boundless energy to be my best self every day.

To the team who support me in my company, Digital Training Institute, and who share my vision for Public Sector Marketing Institute. Your enthusiasm for my ideas never ceases to amaze me.

To my publishing company, Page Two, with whom I have had the pleasure of working. I felt managed, mentored and motivated at every part of this book's journey. You are a force of women to be reckoned with (along with Peter)—just my type of women! Your professionalism and patience are greatly appreciated. To Jesse, Amanda, Emily, Rony, Annemarie, Taysia, Melissa, Michelle, Alison and everyone at Page Two, you made writing a book so easy with your constant guidance and support.

To the public sector marketing pros across the world who work, study and train with me to scale digital communications within their organisation and who want to positively impact the citizens they serve, thank you for choosing me as your mentor and muse. In serving you, I am helping you serve better public interest messaging online.

To my business mentors who have shaped my thinking and helped me get out of my own way to unleash this book, this brand and my potential, I will be forever grateful for your support, accountability, friendship and guidance. To Chris Ducker and Sigrun Gudjonsdottir, this book would not have been a reality without your mentorship and masterminds.

Finally, I want to acknowledge myself. I wrote this book through a divorce; it provided solace and safety and reminded me of who I am, and I too am worthy. I am proud to bring this title to the market and I genuinely hope that it has the transformative impact that I intend it to have.

Go forth and transform from the inside out, so that you serve the great citizens of your town, your city, your region, your state, your country or your continent. Tell stories that resonate and be prepared to have online conversations, no matter how difficult it feels. The world has changed, and we need you to change it for the good, one digital message at a time.

Contents

FOREWORD

THE COVID-19 PANDEMIC massively disrupted our globally inter-connected economy. Generations of researchers will study the impact, attempting to quantify and understand the long-term consequences. Some will look at the positive effects digital commu-nications had in maintaining the flow of critical information in a time of physical isolation.

Without digital technology, the impact of the pandemic would have been considerably worse. Friends and family would not have been able to instantly check in on each other's well-being. Businesses and schools could not have adapted to a remote and virtual operat-ing model. Governments and the media would be hard-pressed to quickly and efficiently share vital public health information.

In the last edition of this book, I shared the following in my foreword:

> Public and private sector organisations that fail to evolve and deliver experiences that their customers expect risk becoming irrelevant.

My years spent in the Obama White House and State Depart-ment were singularly focused on improving how we carried out the duties of providing citizen services. Given the rapid advancement of technology, these days are ancient history in the timeline of digital transformation. Our primary concerns were helping pull the govern-ment into the present with smart mobile devices, Wi-Fi, Bluetooth and cloud-based collaboration technologies to untether employees from their desks. We helped set the foundation of preparedness in the unlikely event of a localised incident disrupting the ability to commute to a centralised work location. Then the world was hit with COVID-19.

The organisations that were able and prepared to operate in a remote manner adapted best in a world that rapidly shut down, closed borders, restricted movement and shifted to an online model of business. Across the world, we saw governments innovating using technology to minimise the impact of the pandemic and continue business operations.

Prior to vaccine availability, contact tracing was the method commonly used by governments to help slow the spread of COVID-19 infections. Singapore's Ministry of Health responded to this need with their TraceTogether mobile app, cutting in half the time taken to isolate infected citizens. Legislative bodies in Brazil, the UK and Latvia adopted rules to permit remote debating and voting using video conferencing platforms. The national health department in South Africa used WhatsApp to share health and testing information with locals, while countering misinformation about 'cures' for coronavirus.

No solution was perfect, and many innovative efforts failed to deliver the desired outcomes. But life continues regardless of global circumstances and the duties of the public sector only expand when faced with significant challenges. Innovating and failing is a sign that people are trying to make things better. That is the definition of what the public sector is supposed to do in providing citizen services. We elect leaders, pay taxes and participate in civil society in the hope that today is better than yesterday.

The biggest impediment to organisational transformation is people. The inability to adapt or evolve will lead to an early death for all ideas. Humans are inherently fallible and the weakest link in any change effort. They are also the strongest force for good when properly skilled and motivated. If you are reading this book, you are already demonstrating your motivation to be better. And, by the end of this book, you should expect to have enhanced skills and capabilities to perform your duties.

Preparation and enablement are key factors in being able to operate under difficult conditions. Bad things happen on a local, national or global scale. We hope they are rare and limited in their impact, but it is part of human history. We do not want to find our government institutions and their employees reacting to situations because that demonstrates a lack of preparedness.

When we are prepared, our organisations enable us to successfully adapt when normal circumstances become abnormal. If we are motivated and encouraged to learn the right skills, we are positioned to appropriately adapt and respond. The difference between responding and reacting is that the latter is an action opposing an initial force, often immediate and rash. Responding is measured, deliberative and calculated, and considers the potential impact of the action. A response is done when you are prepared and enabled with the right skills and resources. It is what we want from governments and large organisations in which we place our trust.

Joanne Sweeney's book is the manual you need to read and refer to so as to remain prepared and properly skilled with critical digital capabilities in your government or public sector role. It is the guidebook I sorely needed when I started at the White House in January 2011; all the lessons I learned took years and countless failures for me to fully grasp. Give yourself a head start and take this book's brilliant ideas and try to make the way services are delivered today a little better than yesterday.

Challenges to the way you operate will rarely be in the form of a global pandemic. Regardless of the challenge, the way you prepare yourself and ultimately respond is how you fulfil the duties and responsibilities of serving the public. Our collective experience from the last few years teaches us that life continues regardless of global circumstances, and the duties of the public sector only expand when faced with significant challenges.

TOM COCHRAN

The White House 2011–2012
US Department of State 2014–2016
thomascochran.com

Leadership in Digital Communications Strategy

Welcome to the post-pandemic age

Now that you have stepped into the shoes of your citizens and become fully fledged digital communicators, are you ready to take the elevator to the next level?

The leadership demonstrated in government and public sector globally in the past two years has been nothing short of transformational. In fact, transformational does not adequately describe the significance of your digital manoeuvres.

In the time since the first edition of this book was published, we have lived through a pandemic and according to Google, digital transformation has been expedited by a decade in two years. We are also witnessing war storytelling on social media from Ukraine. The world is forever changed and communications is ever-changing. How are you adapting and evolving?

COVID-19 has re-written the rules of public sector marketing and I felt compelled to bring this book into the post-pandemic age. The first edition has been heralded by readers as an essential guide, helping them navigate public interest messaging online.

This second edition reflects on the transformation within government and public sector and addresses the massive shifts and overnight agility when the public health crisis shut down the world. It is reflective but reformist in its approach to the new rules of communications in a digital-first world.

The authenticity of the stories and lived experiences that you will learn from helped frame the call to action in this edition. I want this book to be the bible that helps you scale digital communications like never before. This book must find its way into the hands, ears and eyes of non-marketing professionals and managers in all departments of government and public sector. It is time to drive cohesive digital communications to satisfy the Netflixised nations where intent meets innovation.

In the early days of the pandemic in 2020, I began recording weekly YouTube videos and commenting from the communications sidelines. Part of me wanted to tell the story as it would be told by historians, so it felt right to document in-the-moment experiences as I watched how the world responded from a communications perspective.

Let's face it, COVID-19 was a novel coronavirus; nobody had all the answers but the public demanded them. The focus on newsfeeds moved from major retail, beauty and corporate brands that heretofore commanded most of our attention on social media to livestreams of public health and political leaders providing updates on coronavirus.

The eyes of citizens from affected nations were on government and public sector. We looked to them for leadership and answers.

It was very clear from the outset that open, transparent and timely public engagement was needed to keep people indoors, effectively locked down in our homes. With more time on our hands, Digital Age citizens, hungry for information, doubled their time spent online. Meanwhile video messaging on Facebook increased by 70% just one month after the world was plunged into a pandemic. Meta CEO Mark Zuckerberg detailed the changing behaviour in a press briefing in March 2020.

The speed of the spread of COVID-19 was matched by the acceleration of online messaging, social networking and Google searches as citizens tried to find out every possible detail about this virus. Citizens looked for a diverse range of expert views to help them make up their own minds on how deadly this disease was, and how it would ultimately impact their lives.

Those 'experts' were legitimate and not. As I write today we still have states and nations with mass unvaccinated populations, and in the words of the wise World Health Organization, *'nobody is safe until everybody is safe'*.

The digital communications antidote that saved lives

There is one statement that came to me during those early days of COVID-19 as I watched digital communications leadership from government and public health on my smartphone, casting on my smart TV and listening on my smart speaker. I recorded videos and podcasts and reminded the public and public sector pros that digital communications was saving lives. This statement has stayed with me and it is one that I truly believe deserves highlighting in this book and on every platform I have access to.

> 'In the absence of a vaccine, there was only one antidote to COVID-19 and that was effective digital communications whereby citizens heard, understood and acted on public health advice disseminated online and in mainstream media.'

JOANNE SWEENEY, April 2020

The acceleration of COVID-19 through society was matched only by the agility of science to create life-saving vaccines. But it is also true that the dexterity of decision-making by political leaders and senior public servants in our governments and public health departments led to an almost overnight shift from a mainly traditional communications approach with some digital output to a digital-first and in many cases digital-only strategy.

It was imperative, therefore, that I updated this book to reflect the engagement of public sector marketing pros and their broader management teams in digital communications in a pressure-cooker pandemic world.

The second edition of *Public Sector Marketing Pro* revels in the transformation from traditional to full digital strategy.

If digital was part of the communications toolbox pre-COVID, it's now the prerequisite uniform, artillery and defence mechanism to operate in the now.

It's likely a third edition of this book will be required as the pandemic slows and the Metaverse gains traction. Such is the speed of marketing and communications transformation that we must remain agile in a world where change equals relevance.

What can you expect from this edition?

All chapters have been updated and reflect the digital landscape in 2022. An explicit leaning to scaling digital communications flows through all chapters. You will also learn lived lessons from pandemic communications from across the world in a chapter dedicated to those experiences. Finally, there is a new lens on advancing technologies and Web 3.0, as well as the new social media disruptor that is TikTok.

Data and evidence-based content and graphical depictions of rising and falling incidences of coronavirus, hospitalisations and deaths dominated the pandemic news cycle as the world battled a pandemic and an infodemic. We will look at the role that big data plays in digital communications as we shift gears in our marketing and messaging.

It is clear that now or in the future there is no greater currency for government and public sector than trust and transparency. It can be lost in misinformation cycles, but it can be won in showing up online as human, authentic and taking accountability.

I hope you enjoy reading or listening to this book, as much as I have enjoyed writing and recording it. To everyone that has engaged with me on this topic, thank you; your interactions have inspired the words on these pages.

The digital transformation that has taken place in government and public sector agencies over the past two years has reorientated you into well-oiled digital-first communications engines firing on multiple digital channels simultaneously.

If ever a shake-up was needed, we didn't think it would arrive in the form of a global pandemic. Even technology had to catch up with coronavirus.

The knock-on effect was massive in terms of work practices because communications professionals were remote working, as were their colleagues, and previous senior leadership personal bias around the roles of social media, websites and the Internet more generally were completely forgotten. Instead, they asked, 'How do we reach the public and engage them online?'

I use the terms 'government' and 'public sector' interchangeably throughout this book to reflect all types of bodies that have a government remit, so this includes governments and houses of parliament, government departments, public and civil servants, police forces, politicians and political parties, non-profit agencies, state-funded programmes and economic development agencies, semi-state bodies, charitable organisations, tourism, education, health, defence and other similar organisations that are state supported.

* * * * *

THE PUBLIC INTEREST, PREVIOUSLY dictated by civil and public servants, politicians and policy makers, is increasingly in the hands of the people—those the government and civil service are there to serve. It is therefore incumbent on you to step up and scale digital communication skills across your organisation. This book is an aid to that transformation.

1

Scaling Agile Digital Communications

How to scale digital communications in your organisation in a 24/7 mainstream news cycle with infodemic influence

Mainstream media has adapted well to its disruption by social media and search marketing, and its love affair with the public increased during the pandemic as citizens sought out stories and science. All the while the infodemic of misinformation began to rise to the surface of newsfeeds as the world became more divided. The parable of this chapter finds its roots in the ever-changing landscape of news, media and the growing prowess of digital content creators.

As a former broadcast journalist, and a professional that taps into my journalistic toolbox for my everyday work, I am very aware of the changing news landscape and how media ownership is now democratised and in the hands of many. When I reference media, I will be distinct on whether I'm referring to mainstream media, social media, search marketing or social media influencers.

The disciplines of public relations and journalism have never been so important. The need to convince, convert and converse is becoming increasingly difficult as we battle content overload, fake news and a fragmented Internet.

Many PR and marketing pros have embraced digital communications, but how do you transform a whole department or organisation? Being able to pivot so that your traditional communications are agile and fluid in the Digital Age is not just advantageous, it is absolutely necessary. And we must go a step further. The ownership of messaging no longer lies solely with the PR, media or marketing department—it must sit front and centre from its source of truth.

The fact is we need digital communications to become an owned task in each function of government and public sector, driven at the top by the CEO, director or president, led by the communications function and allied by the circle of teams creating content at their desk, with a clear understanding that their work needs to live online.

Digital communications is everyone's responsibility, and subject matter experts need to step up and support the communications function. They can no longer delegate it. You see the spectre of social commentary is such that by your absence online, you are part of the problem, and your presence is very much the solution.

The Joe Rogan Effect and why you should care

The Joe Rogan Effect is a phrase I've coined to describe the rise in influence of non-journalists who are tackling issues that are dominating mainstream news media. On New Year's Eve 2021, YouTube removed a video from the Joe Rogan Experience channel. It was an interview with Dr Robert Malone, who claims that he was part of the team that invented the mRNA vaccine platform. We are all familiar with the term mRNA in a COVID-19 world. But are you aware of Joe Rogan?

Well I was. As a podcaster for many years, Joe Rogan was seen as the one you looked up to in terms of podcasting success. He was the first podcaster to sign an exclusive publishing deal with Spotify in 2020 and his podcasts are among the most listened to in the world. His podcasts are interview-based and he has now published

1,806 episodes (at time of writing) with the controversial one with Dr Malone appearing as number 1,757.

In my view, and as an observer of the changing media and evolving digital landscape, this trend is one to watch in 2022 and beyond, whereby influencers with engaged audiences will continue shaping public opinion and potentially dividing public opinion on critical matters of public health, democracy and other public policy issues.

Chaos, clicks and controversy: understanding the influence commanded by social media influencers

Chaos, clicks and controversy. These are the three Cs of commercial online appeal.

Negativity online spreads faster than positivity and if you want more clicks, emotional writing will act like a magnet when the sentiment is driven by hate, criticism, fear or any other negative emotion.

There are six things public sector and government communications professionals need to understand about the rise of social media influence.

1. Media is a commodity owned by anyone and everyone willing to create content online and traditional media outlets no longer get to control the narrative. Creators are highly sought-after individuals (such as Joe Rogan) and they are building significant influence and attention among their tribe.

2. Understand that influence online can be measured in three ways:

-   The volume of followers you have and the corresponding performance metrics such as reach, impressions, interactions, engagement rate, video views and sentiment

-   An engaged audience that listens, acts and advocates for a particular view, service or product heralded by said influencer

-   When your online content becomes the focus of mainstream media

3. Ignore influencers with social share of voice in your space at your peril because that is to ignore the reality of the public's attention.

4. Dismiss non-mainstream media voices as irrelevant—this is a dangerous mindset as you are becoming part of the infodemic problem by not correcting the record or publishing enough counter-argument content to influence public opinion and insight.

5. Listen to the public discourse and discover knowledge or information gaps that you can fill, and in doing so be an ally to the audiences that seek out the truth.

6. Reframe your communications strategy to reflect the digital era of influence and audit where your gaps are in terms of social listening, influential and authority content and real-time responsiveness.

Digital News Report 2021 and the shift in media consumption and influence

The 2021 Digital News Report conducted by the Reuters Institute in association with the University of Oxford shines a spotlight on why citizens are accessing news on social and who they are interested in listening to and learning from.

In the 10th study, 46 countries comprising 92,000 respondents were surveyed about their news consumption habits.

One section in particular is worth focusing on. Respondents under the age of 35 were asked who they pay most attention to when using social media as a news source. The findings are striking and worth reading at least twice!

The report explores if journalists and news organisations should play a more prominent role on these networks and provide more credible information. Some media organisations have already ventured into this arena. *The Guardian*, for example, produces the 'Fake or for Real?' segment on Instagram, where a young journalist goes over the week's claims using the platform's quiz feature.

Irish journalist Richard Chambers also uses TikTok to update followers on the main political and news agenda of the day.

I want to highlight one specific question asked in this study, namely, 'When using mobile-video social networks Instagram, Snapchat and TikTok to explore news, what sources do you go to first?' Respondents were given the following options:

- Mainstream media outlets/mainstream journalists
- Smaller or alternative news sources
- Politicians/political activists
- Ordinary people
- Internet personalities
- Other/none of these

Across all three social apps, Internet personalities were dominant at 36% on Instagram, 37% on Snapchat and 40% on TikTok. The ever-eroding position of traditional news media must be a red flag for public sector marketing pros and senior leadership and act as a stark reminder that traditional PR tactics must evolve along with your own digital influence as an organisation and the teams within them.

WHO UNDER 35S PAY MOST ATTENTION TO FOR NEWS ON SOCIAL

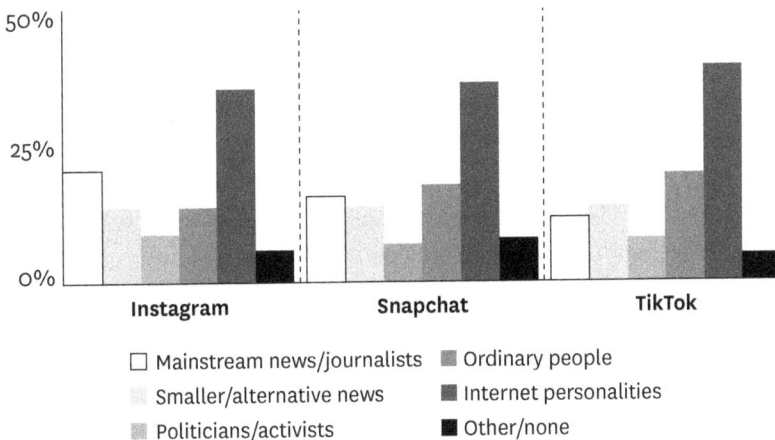

Source: Reuters Institute/University of Oxford

Your social influence is expected by the public

What happens if a Tweet causes a social media storm and hours pass before you are alerted? What happens if your social share of voice on a critical issue is losing ground faster than you can say 'digital transformation'? Well, quite simply, if you are ignoring the speed of digital conversations, you will be chasing the crisis on the back foot. There is no room for the argument 'social media is not relevant for our organisation'—the time for that excuse has long since passed.

Transformation takes time, costs money and requires buy-in from everyone affected. Transformation only works when mindsets shift and work practices evolve, but the rewards of transformation are greater than the effort. Trust me, I've seen it in action with my clients.

When embarking on a new path, the day-to-day operations won't stop and so it can be challenging to find the time, mental bandwidth and even tenacity to keep the wheels of change in motion. But if you are not evolving your communications function to match the speed of digital change, you are slipping backwards to what will feel like snail mail.

The vastness of the communications manager's remit today is daunting. In fact, there are roles in this discipline that didn't exist even two years ago, and I predict additional positions will soon be created. But the team that you have right now is probably made up of instinctive communicators and experienced marketers who can intuit the needs of your government department, public sector agency, law enforcement agency or political party. So, let's not fire the team! Your team will be the driving force, the shoulders to the wheel, the heart and soul of transformation. The first task is to empower them to be the change you want to see in your organisation. The second task is to scale digital communications organisation-wide.

Responding to the communications cycle in a post-pandemic world

The news cycle is no longer controlled by top-of-the-hour bulletins or print deadlines. Always-on media is being driven by the smartphone revolution and the incessant desire for 'right now' information satisfaction. The insatiable attraction of drawing a huge audience means that we have lost sense of tracking real individuals while ensuring we are having meaningful conversations. The combined challenge of serving a 24/7 media and public requires a communications service with shared objectives.

The tactics involved in digital public relations are relatively similar to those of traditional PR; for example, building relationships and securing placements. Digital PR, however, has the added benefit of impacting SEO (search engine optimisation) and link-building across the web. These measurable, digital tactics provide tangible results and insights. Another key differentiator of digital PR is the ability to build connections with bloggers and influencers, who are key players in the digital space.

When you set out on your transformation journey and endeavour to restructure your communications team and introduce new systems, you will need a plan. Very often most of what you need exists, but it is about taking the time to do it right, and bringing the right people with you. Organisations that don't embrace change face being outmanoeuvred by their digital-savvy public sector peers. Even worse, leaders with 'digital snobbery'—who think they don't need to incorporate digital storytelling into their campaigns, for example—will hurt their organisations beyond repair.

Take a moment to consider how you should approach revitalising your traditional communications department into an agile, proactive and socially responsive team. In the rest of this chapter I will map out the actions to enable transformation. Suffice to say, you should customise the detail of each step to suit your own organisation.

Scaling knowledge by building an internal Digital Skills Academy

The very first step of your digital transformation journey is to audit the skillsets available within your marketing and PR department/s. It is likely that you already have social media managers, a website manager and digital content creators who operate in isolation or alongside traditional marketing, press, media and internal communications roles.

Let's face it: all of these roles are communications roles, and you might argue with me as to why I separate them. In my experience, many public sector bodies still divide old and new media, while others have hired a social media manager and layered that over a traditional communications position.

Before we delve into structure and work practices, you need to identify the current skillsets within your department or organisation. I have developed the following model for public sector organisations in order to scale knowledge internally and deliver truly digital-first communications.

The Digital Skills Academy Model

Digital skills audit: Undertake a digital skills audit amongst all communications staff to establish the level of knowledge and expertise in-house.

Digital skills quiz: While you're undertaking the digital skills audit, it is important to identify the depth of knowledge of certain digital marketing disciplines within your team. As part of the audit, develop a digital skills quiz, which will assess their current knowledge against best practice and give them an industry score from 1–100. You can use the glossary of terms in the back of this book as a starting point to develop a quiz that tests existing knowledge.

Identify champions: In true workshop-style, identify digital transformation champions who are first with ideas, first to accept new ways of working and who always show enthusiasm.

Peer-to-peer learning: Develop a model of peer-to-peer learning in-house to help scale knowledge within the organisation as you realise and reinforce that digital is everyone's responsibility. For example, the champions you identified in the previous step can be partnered with colleagues who are lacking digital skills.

In-house events: Digital marketing and social media seminars, conferences or boot camps twice a year will ensure that the digital agenda is prioritised within the organisation.

Masterminds for senior executives: To scale digital transformation across the organisation, it is beneficial for senior leaders to engage in an immersive mastermind experience with like-minded peers from other public sector and government organisations, so they can lead out on the change agenda.

Regular meetings: Holding regular social media, digital transformation and editorial meetings will ensure that everyone involved in a project understands the role of digital. It is also important that digital is not simply pushed onto a digital manager and glossed over in meetings.

Learning materials: Within the Digital Skills Academy there should be updated and live policies, procedures, tutorial videos and templates that staff members can easily access on the job and remotely, possibly in the cloud.

Recognition of learning: To digital-proof your organisation, take ongoing continuing professional development (CPD)–accredited training. I license my Digital Skills Academy to public sector clients, allowing them to scale at speed because they do not have to develop the learning management systems or expert content. When CPD modules are completed by staff members, senior management should recognise this professional learning in some way and the training should be considered in regard to future promotional opportunities.

Setting shared key performance indicators (KPIs)

When you are certain of the skills gaps and how to fill them, you need to set shared KPIs for your communications department. Many departments within public sector organisations work independently of each other. This means that each department has its own KPIs, and while every element of work has a communications remit, the measurement of results does not always include a full cross-departmental report.

Here are some examples of individual team KPIs:

- **Press teams** provide press release output, media monitoring results and advertising value equivalent (AVE) metrics.

- **Internal communications teams** provide updates on staff engagement, intranet statistics and internal cluster metrics.

- **Social media teams** provide reach, engagement and channel growth reports.

- **Marketing teams** provide campaign analysis and traditional advertising data.

- **Website managers** provide analytics based on user sessions, most searched terms, most visited page/s, time on site, bounce rate, goals and conversions.

This structure of individual and fragmented reporting no longer cuts it. It does not join up the digital dots in a world where clicks, shares, likes, comments, opens and downloads reflect the actions of possibly one person. But yet many organisations regard these top-level metrics as success. The question is, do we really know what each KPI means? Can we identify individual citizens amidst a myriad of seemingly random clicks?

Shared KPIs will ensure that the core objectives of the organisation are prioritised while also serving the public in the world of fast-moving digital communications.

For example, one key objective for a police force over a 12-month period may be to build up trust amongst the public after a series of internal crises that dominated media headlines during the previous quarter. The communications department makes a structured and sustained effort to engage in digital storytelling supported by traditional PR and marketing activities. Here are the activities and associated KPIs that might apply to this entire project:

- **Public relations:** Positive media mentions and interviews (radio, TV, print, online) and trust marketing PR output.

- **Marketing:** Trust marketing campaign output and specific results.

- **Website:** Site keyword search analysis.

- **Social media:** Cross-channel sentiment analysis.

- **Digital PR:** Backlinks to community pages and increased traffic.

- **Email marketing:** Sign-ups to new community e-zine.

- **Internal communications:** Engaging officers nationwide to provide anecdotal evidence and case studies of on-the-ground citizen engagement, with priorities pursued and achieved.

- **Citizen survey:** Results of public trust research.

In order to assess the impact of this combined traditional and digital marketing outreach, the police force's communications team needs to set shared KPIs for success within a set timeframe.

Considering the strengths of your internal communications team

You must review your internal communications structure across all communications disciplines. Do they meet only when they need to? Do they have defined and shared KPIs? Do they delegate amongst heads of department? How is work prioritised and who has the power to decide what is done and when? If there is internal strife around tasks and projects, this will filter out and negatively impact your external communications.

Streamlined communications amongst heads of department is vital, along with a shared understanding of each other's work and team dynamic. In reforming your communications function, you will need to identify synergies, fragmented work practices and opportunities for efficiencies.

Assessing roles and titles

Many job descriptions are out of date. They simply do not take into account digital communications tasks (whether or not these tasks are being done). Here is a list of job functions that you would expect to find in an agile digital communications department. The size of the department or organisation will dictate the scale of the skills you have. Of course, some of these tasks may be done by more than one person, or outsourced to digital agencies, and these divisions of labour should be taken into account:

- Social media manager
- Facebook account manager
- Twitter account manager
- Instagram account manager
- TikTok account manager
- YouTube account manager
- LinkedIn account manager
- Snapchat account manager
- Pinterest account manager
- Community manager
- Digital content creator
- Copywriter
- Digital content editor
- Keyword and competitor researcher
- Analytics manager
- Email marketer
- Social listening manager

- Social media crisis manager
- Digital designer (web, social, email)
- Video editor
- Video producer
- Blogger/social news reporter
- Funnel manager
- CRM manager
- Social customer service team
- Web customer service team
- Search engine optimisation manager
- Search advertising manager
- Social media advertising manager
- Digital PR manager
- Chatbot developer
- UX (user experience) designer
- UI (user interface) designer
- Website manager
- Digital governance manager
- Data protection officer

Rolling out your next public sector campaign

There are several factors to consider before rolling out a digital communications campaign. These include:

Workflows

When job descriptions are updated and digital communications roles are divided amongst your team (existing and/or new), it is time to assess new workflows. Very often I see overlap or, worse, gaps in digital communications when people step back from seemingly mundane tasks.

It must be noted that the smallest of digital tasks is usually very important. Take, for example, tagging your blog posts on your website. It seems not so important, but post tags are used for granular classifications. Think of them like a book's index—tags should help visitors find information that your blog often covers.

In order to understand the remit of all team members, it is useful to start a project or campaign that involves everyone with a communications role. This project can be your benchmark to test your workflows, and can help demonstrate how multiple communications functions are required to deliver a successful public sector marketing campaign.

Work plans

Within your team, determine how long it will take to roll out a public sector campaign, and then break down the tasks by hours or days. Here is a sample workflow, based on the 37-hour working week of a public sector marketing pro (who will have other tasks to complete along with these).

TASKS	HOURS
Reporting	2
Content creation	8
Content calendar design	1
Content scheduling	3
Campaign management	4
Social advertising management	6
Community management	4
Online PR	3
Training	1.5
Reporting and data analysis	3.5
Continuing professional development (CPD)	1

Budget

Transformation requires long-term investment. Since digital is always evolving, a rolling investment, not a defined budget, is required. Bear in mind that remaining stagnant will cost more in the medium- to long-term.

Content

New skills and work practices are needed to meet the content demands of search and social. Chapter 5 outlines the recent and ongoing transformation of content.

Software

Software as a service (SaaS) and technology will support the evolution of digital communications and create efficiencies, as machine learning completes tasks much more quickly and accurately than humans.

* * * * *

DIGITAL TRANSFORMATION IS HAPPENING across all facets of public life. It is not a case of 'if we' embrace digital transformation in the public sector; conversations should be happening now around 'what steps do we need to take to be digitally robust?' Public sector communications is now firmly in the hands of the public as their voice influences the media, politicians and, of course, each other. The days of using the media as a buffer are over. Citizen journalists, whether we like it or not, are power brokers in the Digital Age. They are influencers of public policy and media narrative. At a time when trust in our institutions is higher than in recent years due to the pandemic, and the reliance on our government and public sector agencies to inform, support, legislate and empower citizens, there is a real opportunity to narrow the public trust gap further.

Our lives are changing quickly, and so are the ways we communicate with each other. Old ways of engaging with the public are becoming increasingly out of date; this became evident over the past two years. But is the public sector able to scale and automate, and, more importantly, is it willing to? That's the biggest challenge facing your organisation today.

Customising Your Communications Strategy in the Digital Age

How has citizen behaviour changed in the post-pandemic age?

As a communications professional with a responsibility to meet the needs of citizens, you must first step into their shoes to understand how their behaviour is changing in a mostly digital world.

Human nature may be constant at its core, but the behaviour that shapes it is always changing. Ongoing evolution of technology has led to widespread changes in behaviour that accumulate into larger trends. A 20-year-old browsing the web today will behave very differently from their counterpart 10 years ago. Today we are an experiment in a new world called the Metaverse where augmented reality, virtual reality and smart glasses allow us to communicate and engage like never before. At Facebook's annual conference, Connect 2021, CEO Mark Zuckerberg introduced Meta, which brings together their apps and technologies under one new company brand. According to the company, '*Meta's focus will be to bring the metaverse to life and help people connect, find communities and grow businesses.*'

Virtual reality and augmented reality have been mainstream for some years, however the Metaverse will take these technologies into our everyday lives in the coming years. It is the next iteration of the Internet.

Digital transformation in the public sector is about harnessing existing knowledge, leveraging new technologies, having conversations omni-channel and being accessible to demanding Digital Age citizens with social customer service.

Naturally, most of the communication shifts we are currently experiencing are digital. Having instant access has given us the opportunity to find more information, and faster, than ever before. Citizens are now more empowered, informed and action-orientated. The pandemic provided a taster for public interest messaging that was timely, accessible and engaging. These new trends bring with them potentially significant implications for public sector organisations. Let's take a closer look at how citizen behaviour is changing in this decade, and what that might mean for your role and your organisation.

1. Increasing reliance on technology

The Age of Technology, the Digital Age, the Algorithmic Age, Web 3.0, the Metaverse—these terms have become so common, they are part of our everyday vernacular. But that doesn't diminish the fact that we're using and relying on technology to a greater degree than ever before, and that reliance is showing no signs of slowing.

Consider global Internet use. According to a DataReportal study, there were *4.9 billion* Internet users in the world by December 2021. That's over 60% of the world's population. New users are growing at an annual rate of 4.8%, equating to an average of more than 600,000 each day.

Mobile devices are a major reason for that jump. According to Statista, the number of mobile phone users worldwide today surpasses six billion and is forecast to further grow by several hundred million in the next few years. China, India and the United States are the countries with the highest number of smartphone users.

We are living through the smartphone revolution, where decisions are made and actions taken in record time because of record Internet speeds and the free availability of Wi-Fi and free messaging apps such as WhatsApp, Messenger, Telegram, WeChat and Signal.

Technology and the Internet are becoming more accessible. Even countries without strong traditional infrastructure are becoming digitally agile, with low-bandwidth apps such as WhatsApp becoming increasingly popular. Africa, for instance, is home to regions with some of the fastest-growing Internet and smartphone rises over the last few years. Elon Musk's Starlink broadband project is providing satellite connectivity from space. Using advanced satellites in low orbit, Starlink enables video calls, online gaming, streaming and other high-data Internet activities. Google is also scaling work on a project to help the next billion users (NBU) come online in developing countries. They intend to create an Internet that loads in two to three seconds anywhere in the world.

So, with greater access comes greater usage. It is now difficult to imagine a world without Internet access. In fact, this increasing reliance on technology informs many of the trends discussed throughout this book.

2. Democratisation of decision-making

Thanks in large part to that increased technology access, we are now far away from a world of linear communications. Gone are the days when organisations transmitted information to citizens, relying on their credibility to get results. Instead, citizen behaviour has become significantly more democratic, and public sector bodies have to work harder to build trust and buy-in.

We all have technology access, we all have opinions, and we are not afraid to share them. That is why reviews by consumers have become perhaps the single biggest influencer of buying decisions across the globe. Users of public services are writing reviews every day on social media whether you choose to look at them or not. This changed behaviour should be front and centre of your digital communications strategy. In his book *Socialnomics*, Erik Qualman describes social media as word-of-mouth marketing on steroids—such is the reliance on our peers for online reviews. On Facebook, for example, we have on average about 338 friends, according to Pew Internet Research. The cumulative reach of a public sector review (positive or negative) on Facebook could be the equivalent to the listenership of a regional radio station. Which platforms are citizens using to recommend your public services?

We've reversed the more traditional communications model of sender to receiver. Organisations, as a result, have lost leverage. Public sector bodies that are willing and able to work directly with citizens for efforts like user-generated content (UGC) are building a competitive edge and seeing results.

3. The power of the silently informed citizen

One significant trend that public sector organisations need to be aware of is the 'silently informed citizen'. Because citizens no longer have to rely on large companies or public sector organisations for their information, they are no longer raising their hand to get it. As a result, even an active organisation may not know its potential audience before they actually engage with them. That, in turn, has significantly disrupted the traditional audience funnel.

By 10 a.m. there are one billion searches on Google. Citizens are information obsessed and have access to the answers they need at any time. Are you providing those answers via your digital channels?

The average citizen's media journey is becoming less linear, with fewer vertical interactions between audience and organisation and more horizontal interactions between various individuals online. That, in turn, results in significantly more educated citizens, who—thanks to their access to technology—have more information than ever before to make an informed decision.

The Public Sector Marketing Funnel

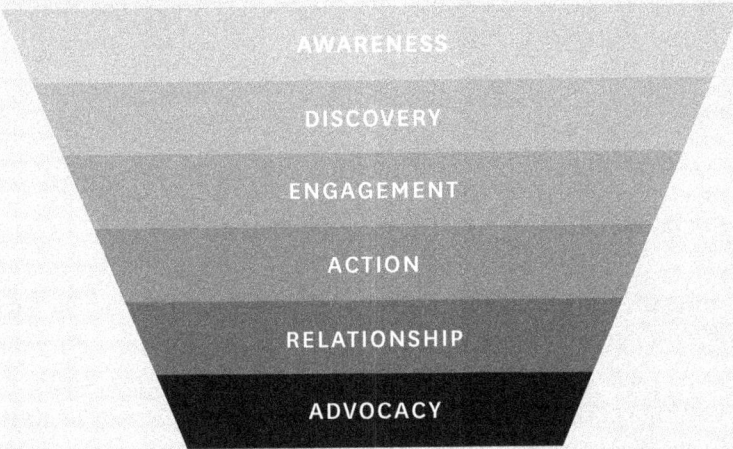

AWARENESS

DISCOVERY

ENGAGEMENT

ACTION

RELATIONSHIP

ADVOCACY

This funnel model presents a visual representation of how organisations attract and retain citizens with digital marketing and communications tactics.

Awareness: At this stage of the funnel, the audience at large is becoming aware of your campaign or messaging. Social media and search marketing are driving this brand awareness.

Discovery: Moving down the funnel, citizens are discovering more about what you are saying. Conversational content, such as video marketing and blogs, drives this engagement.

Engagement: Now that the audience is going deeper into your funnel and spending longer engaging with your content, they are considering what you have to say and if they will respond to your call to action.

Action: This is the sweet spot of the funnel, where the citizen knows, likes and trusts you, and has taken an action or had a conversion on one of your online channels.

Relationship: A digital relationship has been established, and the citizen is probably in your email database and hears from you on a regular basis.

Advocacy: True online advocates are those who share your content and are willing to recommend you and your organisation to their peers online. They are very influential and should be nurtured.

4. Social media as a core communications tool

It's now difficult to imagine a world in which platforms like Facebook, Instagram, TikTok, Twitter, WhatsApp, YouTube and Snapchat don't play a daily role in our lives. Four and a half billion people are now using social networks, and in response public sector organisations are changing how they use social media. They are aware that they must be active on social networks where key audience segments are active so as to be relevant and reachable. They are being more thoughtful about which platforms to use, especially for private messaging, and they are cognisant of governance and privacy issues that dominate the digital world.

A study by Pew Research Center found that social media use increased and it became an important enabler in human connection during multiple lockdowns, from video calls to vaccine registrations, to watching mainstream media and government updates, to researching new ways to stay entertained and shopping online. The vast majority of adults surveyed in the US (90%) said the Internet had been at least *important* to them personally during the pandemic. The share who said it had been *essential*—58%—was up slightly from 53% in April 2020. There was also increases in the number of people who said the Internet had been essential in the past year among those with a bachelor's degree or more formal education, adults under 30, and those 65 and older.

5. Customised content delivered on demand

Increasing availability of technology also means less streamlined content. For decades, much of the world lived in linear communication patterns. We listened to what was on the radio at a given time, read the book in front of us and watched TV shows as they aired. Everything was done in linear steps based on a programming schedule. We fitted our lives around those schedules.

This is not the reality anymore. The Netflix, Spotify and YouTube effect of content distribution is now the norm as most people refuse to be restricted to a schedule. We have effectively shifted to an on-demand culture. We expect content that reflects our personal interests and our needs to be delivered to us. We consume that content exactly when we have time for it, so public sector organisations need to ask themselves if they are customer-centric in their approach to content creation and dissemination.

In addition to this on-demand trend, we are seeing an increasing fragmentation of content. Content is no longer the sole occupation of media and publishing houses; content is now a commodity owned by those who create it. We are all publishers with the right to win eyeballs and retain their attention, which means increased commercial opportunity in the private sector and increased influence potential in the public sector.

Influencers are here because they create content that did not already exist and that resonates with a large audience base. Essentially, they filled a vacuum on the Internet.

Today, you can find any type of content to feed your niche interests. From blogs to podcasts, Facebook Groups to Twitter Spaces, TikTok videos to YouTube videos, whatever you want to know, you can satisfy your need without having to worry that this need has to fit into what everyone else wants at the same time.

6. Visual content as a core communications tool

Human beings have always been visual communicators, and 90% of the information we process is visual. Now, thanks to rapidly advancing technology, we can actually accommodate that need through interactive video, augmented reality, virtual reality, graphics and images. The Digital Content Institute declared 2017 the Year of Visual Content Marketing after rightly predicting that, by 2020, more than 80% of the entire Internet would consist of video.

Citizens in 2022 are no longer pleasantly surprised when they see a video; they expect it. TikTok is a social video app; Instagram has declared it is now predominantly a mobile-video app. Organisations across the world are transforming their social media presence specifically to account for this trend. If you want to get your message across, dynamic and visual communications is absolutely key.

7. The need for instant response and gratification

As consumers, we all share a common theme: we want our information personalised, we need it to be authentic, we prefer it to be visual—and we need it now. That need for instant gratification is the final significant shift in citizen behaviour since 2010.

This change especially manifests itself in customer service. One 2014 study, for instance, found that when users express a question or concern to a brand on Twitter, they expect a response within an hour. According to a study conducted in 2017, taking longer than five minutes to respond to a new lead will decrease customer conversion rates by up to 80%. Consumers are citizens, and whether they are seeking new shoes or health-related content, they won't hang around for you.

Making the need for spontaneity more challenging is the fact that, in addition to needing a quick answer, your audience also wants it to be personalised. A generic boilerplate letting them know that you are looking into their concern is no longer enough. You need to provide human and personalised answers.

Your response should be instant, but it also needs to be customised enough to make the citizen on the other end feel like their unique situation is taken seriously. Speedy social customer service responses that are personalised and specific is the challenge public sector bodies must respond to in the post-pandemic age. Wait five minutes and your service user is already unhappy. Ignore the public at your reputational peril. They are likely to call you out on it—on social media.

8. The explosion of social video

The pandemic catapulted TikTok from the shadows into the social media limelight taking swaths of market share from the big hitters of Facebook, Instagram and YouTube. Instagram re-designed its app interface and introduced its own short video format called Reels. Facebook now supports Reels and users can also cross-post them from Instagram. The TikTok explosion made it the number one downloaded app in 2021 with 656 million downloads—and it shows no signs of slowing. We will discuss this in more detail in the next chapter.

* * * * *

UNDERSTAND THAT CONSUMER BEHAVIOUR has changed forever, and the balance of power is now in the public's hands. You can still be in control from a communications standpoint, but only if you are creating content that answers their questions, and only if you have a customer service response mechanism that is digitally enabled and personalised. You have to be willing to be front of screen to share your authentic voice.

A digital communications strategy for government and public sector

How you communicate with the public is critical. Digital communications has made it easier than ever to interact with citizens, but in some cases, it has made it too easy. You can release statements and spread information with a few clicks, but digital information, once shared, is very difficult to take back. You need an effective digital communications plan that will help govern how you interact digitally.

Step 1: A measurement framework

Begin by creating an outline of exactly what the plan is designed to achieve and why it is important to your organisation. Be specific, and think of this outline as your statement of purpose. What are you hoping to accomplish with your digital communications plan?

Is your goal to:

- Engage more effectively with the public in your community?

- Improve individual understanding of specific concepts related to your work?

- Spread the word about specific public interest information that the public need to know and understand?

- Raise awareness and get engagement on a specific campaign?

- Encourage behaviour change relating to public health or policing, or due to a new piece of legislation?

- Increase voter participation in elections?

When you know what you are trying to accomplish with your digital communications plan, you will be able to shape the rest of the plan accordingly, ensuring that it has all of the key elements you need.

Step 2: Audit existing digital communications activities

Before you create your digital communications plan, take a look at your existing digital communications infrastructure and outputs with a comprehensive digital audit. Evaluate what you already have in place. Do you have social media profiles, a website, active ad campaigns, email marketing or a chatbot that is intended to help raise awareness about specific issues? What are the monthly metrics and how do they compare to other public sector organisations in your jurisdiction?

Be sure to ask:

- **What are you getting right?** What elements of your digital communications are working well for your office? Are you able, for example, to get information out quickly during a crisis? Do you have a large social media following, or strong monthly web traffic? All of these elements can be highly positive, making it easier to connect with your audience.

- **Where are you missing the mark?** Your last ad campaign failed to sway public opinion or raise awareness about a specific issue. You're struggling to figure out how to interpret data from your digital platforms. Maybe your digital communications activities have been sporadic? Whatever the case, make sure that you clearly identify the improvements that you want to make.

- **How does your existing strategy need to change?** Perhaps your digital communications approach needs to shift gears in order to keep up with the changing needs of your organisation, your audience is getting younger and you need to adapt your channel strategy or perhaps there are new voter or citizen needs? It does not necessarily mean that you are doing anything wrong; it just means that changes demand that you pivot how you interact with specific audiences on various platforms. So ask yourself, 'What changes do we need to make?'

Step 3: Define your audience persona

Have you created a specific persona and developed a tone of voice in your digital communications plan? When you think of creating social media posts, writing blogs or designing your website, to whom are you speaking? As a government agency or public sector body, you may have a wide target audience that covers a large age range, all genders and a wide variety of incomes. Or, depending on your office and what you deal with every day, you may be able to narrow your audience substantially. Defining your audience is important both for crafting your posts and for controlling ad visibility. Don't pay for ads that won't reach your target audience!

Just as the goal of a business is to create a digital communications strategy that focuses on their customers, your goal as a government agency should be to provide information that is genuinely beneficial for citizens in your area who are impacted by your policies, procedures and information. Make sure you are asking yourself the following key questions as you define your audience:

- **Who are we hoping to reach?** Are there, for example, specific age ranges that are relevant to your campaign? Do you need to speak to the general population, parents with children in a specific age range or voters in a targeted demographic?

- **What is the geographic location impacted by our organisation?** Some organisations have a wide geographic area of impact, even nationwide. Others may only need to work with local citizens. Defining your audience persona makes targeting your ads a much more effective process.

- **Are there particular interests that are relevant to the citizens we need to communicate with most?** This might, for example, include farming and fishing, education, business or tourism, depending on your agency and what it controls.

Step 4: Fill in the key elements

Your digital communications plan is designed to help shape the way you communicate with the public. Missing any of the key elements may result in a struggle to communicate more effectively with your audience/s. Make sure that your plan includes:

- **Your social media platforms.** Which social media platforms does your office focus most heavily on, and which platforms would you like to adopt? This platform focus will definitely shift over time as your citizen voice evolves and their opinions change. Keep in mind that your office likely can't keep up with every available social media platform, so you should focus on the ones that are most important to your organisation and most relevant to the

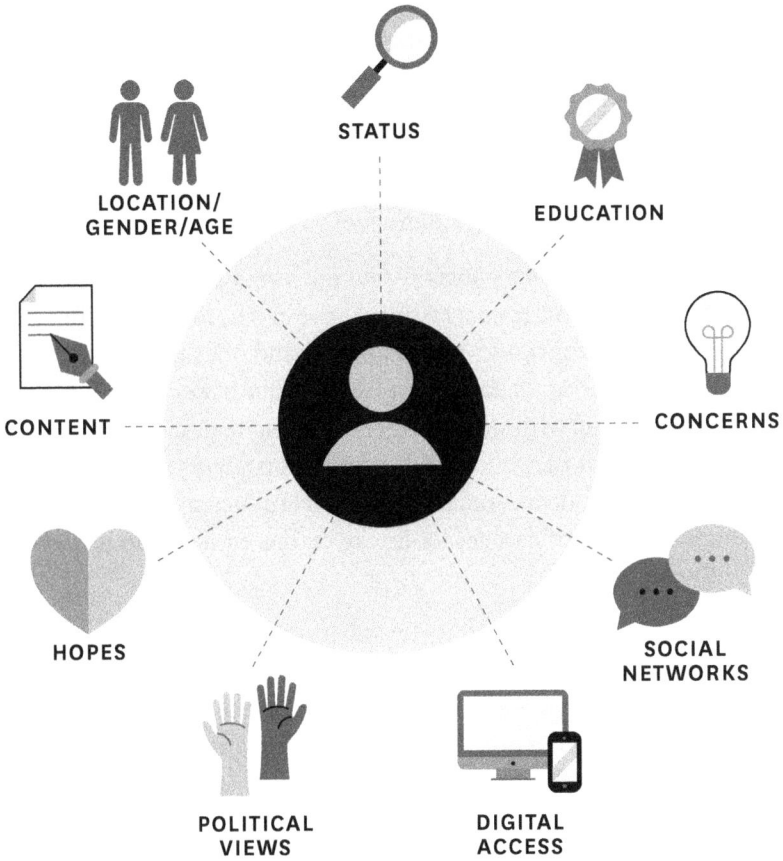

YOUR CITIZEN AVATAR

STATUS

LOCATION/
GENDER/AGE

EDUCATION

CONTENT

CONCERNS

HOPES

SOCIAL
NETWORKS

POLITICAL
VIEWS

DIGITAL
ACCESS

public you serve. For example, the majority of users still have a Facebook account. Younger users, however, are more frequently turning to TikTok, Instagram and YouTube for their information needs, which may mean that you need to start thinking about how to shift your marketing and communications efforts.

- **Your ad campaigns.** Where are you going to focus your advertising efforts? This may include specific messages that you need to communicate on a regular basis. Make sure to include your advertising budget, including a budget range for individual campaigns. You may also want to think about where you are going to target those ads: On social media? Through Google Ads? Where are you most likely to meet your target audience?

- **Your email marketing efforts.** What does your email list look like? Where do you collect new names for your list, including both the names that are given to you voluntarily and ones that may be part of a larger voting or campaign list? Is your data collection strategy compliant with data protection laws, such as the GDPR in Europe? What message do you want to share via your email lists? This may include awareness campaigns to increase public knowledge about specific issues, or it may be a monthly communication with your list.

- **Your platform.** When do you want to send out an email to your users versus communicating with them on social media? Do you require a response, for example, when you're hoping to collect data from your audience, or is it enough to simply put it out there? How will you be collecting that key data and storing it? Does it comply with data protection laws?

- **Information that may be shared across multiple platforms.** For example, you might create a blog post, highlight it on your website, share it across social media and even run an advertising campaign to help increase awareness. However, it is important to clearly define these steps so that you will know how to more effectively share your information.

- **Your persona.** It is important to the public, who are familiar with your work, that you offer them the same, consistent experience across every platform where they communicate with you. You should use the same voice on your social media accounts that you use in your regular email communications, in your advertisements and on other online channels. Your followers want to know what to expect when they communicate with you. While there may be circumstances in which you need to break your persona—in order to share information quickly during a crisis or emergency, for example—you will find that it is much more effective to create a single, solid persona for all of your digital communications.

- **Your SEO effort.** Your SEO strategy is critical to ensuring that you are able to spread the information that citizens need. When people search for information about the topics that are most important to your organisation, you should be at the top of the search engine rankings. You probably put a lot of effort into communicating accurate, trustworthy information, and you'd rather the public came to you for that information than come up with it on their own. Unfortunately, Google and other search engines won't automatically prioritise your site—that's where SEO comes in. What keywords are important for your efforts? What information do you most want to share with your audience, and why is it most important that reliable information comes from you, rather than allowing people to gather misinformation from other sources?

* * * * *

THERE IS NO DOUBT that digital transformation for public sector marketing pros and senior leadership in government is a challenge, ranging from organisational buy-in to upskilling and adapting to new work practices. The greatest challenge of all, however, is the evolution of citizen behaviour and their incredible hunger for immediate information across social and search.

Establishing where your organisation is now in terms of digital communications is key to how you improve and pivot over the coming 12 months. Get your communications team together and design your own plan.

Make your first steps to transformation *willingness* and *enthusiasm*. All the knowledge you need is out there, as are the technologies and platforms. This book is packed with guidance. Bring your people with you and transform from the inside out. Value the experience and marketing skills of your existing staff, but invest time and resources in helping them to develop their digital skills.

How Government Agencies and the Public Sector Can Influence Public Opinion Using Social Media

Leveraging social media to change public opinion on matters of critical public interest

Very often, public sector marketing pros find themselves in the midst of a communications or organisational challenge that is of critical importance and in the public interest. During this time, you will likely be dealing with the media and responding to public concern, and your organisation may be in flux.

In this chapter I want you to understand how social media can be your friend when you put a razor-sharp focus on one prime objective. I also want to give you the confidence to truly engage with the public in order for them to understand your perspective and the public interest message you are trying to communicate.

I do understand that as a government or public sector agency it is important to be careful and conservative, and you may be in the position of having a lot of confidential and proprietary information.

However, you are in the business of public interest messaging, and the public are quite demanding of government agencies. Right now, trust is the number one currency for government agencies in the Digital Age.

Social media for public engagement

By their very nature, public sector and government agencies are largely conservative, cautious and considered when it comes to social media—understandable, given the sensitivities around particular topics and/or management styles. However, there are times when a proactive, forthright yet measured approach to social media is needed to help realise a communications or organisational goal. This was demonstrated throughout the pandemic with press conferences livestreamed on Facebook, Twitter and YouTube.

Social media serves not just your organisation, but also the public interest. You have a responsibility to leverage the channels to reach key audiences and deliver important messages. I challenge you, senior leaders and marketing and communications pros, to put the needs of the public ahead of your own personal bias or reluctance around social media.

10 ways social media can be used for public engagement

1. Targeted communications: deliver the right message to the right audience

The delight of social media communications is our ability to serve very relevant messages to a specific audience, tapping into their needs, wants, fears or desires. We can also use these platforms to find our ideal audience and then direct them to our websites for more detailed information.

EXAMPLE: A new transport route will impact 50,000 commuters in your city. You are obliged to give details of the new route, once you are certain of the specifics. Your communications must start with an awareness campaign so that those directly impacted will realise they must tune in. By using targeted messaging and advertising, you will be able to capture the cohort of people to whom you want to speak. The initial messaging will be informative and should emphasise how the new transport route will impact or benefit their daily commutes.

Using Facebook advertising, you can target people by geography and test a number of different ad formats along with your creative and copy. Then, host more in-depth detail of your messaging on your website and use social to drive the public there so they can better inform themselves. Finally, measure reach, engagement and click-through rates (CTR) to your website landing page.

2. Filter-free communications: talk directly to your audience without the need for a social media intermediary

When I was a journalist, I had the power to decide whether to air a press release that came into our newsroom, or to bin it. The media was a key conduit to the public in the '90s and early noughties and it felt like journalists held all the power. I then jumped the communications fence into public relations and spent many years pitching the media. Today, I have direct online conversations with relevant audiences I want to speak to, and so can you.

When you want to target a specific audience around a public sector campaign, you have the ability to do so via a range of social networks. Going front of screen (as a pre-recorded video or a live-stream) allows you to engage your perfect audience segment.

It has never been easier to get a captive audience. Yes, social media is noisy, yes, it takes time, but consider the outcomes for your campaigns when you have a specific cohort of the public taking note and/or taking action based on your messaging.

EXAMPLE: A PR crisis has escalated online and your organisation is in the midst of a serious communications campaign to win public trust. The media are driving one specific angle, which is distracting from the real issue at hand. Your director arranges a live broadcast on Twitter, giving 60 minutes' notice to the media (via email and Twitter) and also to the public (via Twitter and Facebook). The objective of this broadcast is:

- To give notice that you are going live, which immediately changes the media narrative, as 'the broadcast' becomes the story.

- To get a captive audience listening, which can be very difficult when your news is filtered by the media.

- To provide reassurance and answers.

3. Counteract fake news: your truth needs a digital footprint

'Fake news' became the official *Collins English Dictionary* word of the year for 2017. While Donald Trump may claim to have coined it, propaganda, spin, counter-information, slander and defamation have always been around. I studied these disciplines as a student journalist in 1999. Trust marketing is very important in the Digital Age as we battle fake news and echo chambers. It is your responsibility to counteract fake news. It is hugely damaging to allow untruths and misrepresentations to fly around the social web, causing confusion and perhaps even instilling fear among the public.

When a politician makes a statement in any government house (parliament, senate, Dáil) and they are questioned on the veracity and accuracy of that statement, they may be asked to withdraw it, such is the seriousness of leaving a falsehood on the record. When a newspaper prints an article with errors, they are bound to correct the record by printing an apology and/or a correction. The same principle must apply online.

EXAMPLE: A national health service is experiencing a low uptake of a vaccine because of a campaign by parents suggesting the vaccine causes serious side-effects. It is in the public interest for the health body to communicate the scientific evidence to support its use. Expert voices need to be heard across social media. Engaging the support of the media to help quell fears and correct misinformation is vital.

4. Trust matters: accountability and credibility are key currencies in the post-pandemic age

Trust is the number one currency for public sector organisations and governments today. If you lose the trust of your citizens, you will need to fight hard to win back their hearts and minds.

Whether you are in a position of regaining or maintaining trust, it is vital to have a consistent flow of information on the hard subjects in your social media content plan. Having a senior leader support the corporate accounts is a good idea. Your logo alone will not win public trust. The public want to see an individual speak to them directly, and answer questions.

It is fair to say you won't please all of the people all of the time, but you will reassure them that you are being accountable and continuously working on their behalf.

EXAMPLE: A cyber-security breach has rendered your systems defunct until the source of the hack is identified. Your service users are concerned about the security of their data. While you don't know the source of the issue or the extent, you go live on Facebook and Twitter to reassure citizens that an expert team will be working 24/7 to resolve the issue. You launch an emergency phone line along with a live blog and a crisis hashtag across social media to answer questions in real time with a commitment to update the public once new information comes to hand. You also enlist the expertise of external consultants to provide supplementary knowledge if there are gaps, and you ask them to engage in planned and structured online conversations to quell fears.

5. Measure impact: understand who is engaging with your content

When we get media coverage on a radio station, on TV or in a newspaper, we have access to demographic information that includes gender, geography and age profile. However, we are limited on the detail of who engaged with our messages and why.

Stepping online, we get more meaningful data around engagement. When somebody engages with our content, the type of metrics we can expect include who clicked, viewed, shared, downloaded, subscribed and commented—plus how often, at what time and on what device. We also get more insightful data around the profile of our audiences, such as marital status, occupation, interests, meta location, retention rate and new or returning visitor.

EXAMPLE: A national tourism agency promoting the coastal region as a surfing destination will have a specific audience segment in mind. While they may invest in printed advertising in an outdoor magazine, there is a major opportunity to engage directly with this audience online. A content marketing plan that speaks to avid surfers will allow the tourism marketing staff to measure who and how many qualified leads are engaging with their content.

Tactics deployed may include:

- An epic blog post of 2,000 words describing the top 10 surfing destinations in Ireland, to measure unique readers, time on the page, bounce rate, age, gender, device, location and referral traffic source.

- The ultimate guide to packing for your surfing holiday, to qualify leads by collecting email addresses and measuring click-through rates (CTR) and email subscribers.

- A YouTube video with a surfing world champion (embedded on your website landing page) on how to prepare for a weekend surfing expedition, to measure video views, retention rate, location, age, gender and device.

6. Shape public opinion: influence the narrative and win public support

Frank Jefkins came up with the Transfer Process, and it is a model that I continually go back to in my work. Through effective communications, the digital PR practitioner can convert the four negative attitudes of the public into four positive attitudes.

JEFKINS'S TRANSFER PROCESS

Hostility → Sympathy
Apathy → Interest
Prejudice → Acceptance
Ignorance → Knowledge

While Jefkins developed this framework for traditional public relations, I believe it has a strong role in Digital Age communications. This model allows the organisation to respond to available information in an effective manner. This approach taps into the emotional psyche of your audience/s, and can be used to change perceptions on particular topics or brands. For instance, when you develop a campaign that includes the audience you want to engage, you are merely a facilitator and the audience becomes the advocates.

EXAMPLE: Voter registration among 18–21-year-olds is at an all-time low and the government needs to inspire young people to register to vote. You launch a social media campaign to highlight the value of your democratic vote. The strategy is centred on peer-to-peer voices. A group of 18–21-year-olds go front of screen to share their insights into why they are so passionate about voting. The content is shared via a six-part YouTube show, with promotion and call-to-watch snippets shared on Instagram Stories.

CASE STUDY: Ireland's Youth Become More Politically Engaged

THERE IS A real-life example that perfectly sums up how electoral apathy was transformed into massive interest, where planes full of young people returned to Ireland to vote in the marriage equality referendum of 2015. The hashtag #hometovote trended for days as people felt compelled to digitally document their reasons and deep desires to vote. It was also the first time that a state legalised same sex marriage through a popular vote of the people.

In total, 1.2 million people voted in favour of changing the Irish constitution to allow for same sex marriage. The Yes vote prevailed by 62% to 38%, with a 60.5% turnout.

Source: thejournal.ie

7. *Knowledge transfer: social media drives*
traffic to the web, where the real story awaits

It is a myth to suggest that long-form content is dead. In fact, consumers are curious to an extent that you may not believe. Researching everything, no matter how small, is the norm. The team at Think with Google have been analysing the search habits of its users, and they found that consumers 'use search throughout the decision-making journey to get advice on purchases, even a toothbrush or an umbrella. This means there's an opportunity for marketers to influence across categories.'

So, how does this use of search tools affect public interest messaging for government and public sector agencies? Quite simply, you have never had more of a responsibility to communicate digitally.

With people most inclined to Google an answer to their question, the balance of power lies with those creating the content and tuning into audience needs. There is a real and urgent need to publish public interest content on the Internet that will inform and empower citizens on matters they deem important.

If government and public sector bodies feel less than inclined to invest in content marketing, they are leaving the Internet door wide open for bloggers, YouTubers, influencers and, let's face it, fake news hacks to capture the attention and influence of citizens. If you fail to digitally tell the story, share the message, document the journey or publish the research, you are in danger of not only allowing but in fact, in my opinion, contributing to fake news.

Your apathy to engage with the public online is in effect supporting bad actors on the Internet.

EXAMPLE: Veganism is growing in popularity among young women. A state food agency wants to inform young women about the need to have a varied diet in order to maintain good health. After undertaking significant keyword research on Google, the agency realises that share of voice around veganism lies in the hands of influencers and brands with a market interest. They set out to rank for the top 10 keywords in Google in their country and leverage their knowledge, scientific research and expertise in their ecosystem. They publish a 10-part YouTube video series complemented by optimised blog posts, which attract organic traffic. With a planned 16-week strategy of content marketing and promotion, they narrow the gap in social share of voice and realise that the knowledge they have is the answer to many of their public trust issues.

8. Build advocates: citizens share your content on their own social networks

User-generated content (UGC) is valuable and powerful, and it intrinsically shapes public opinion. UGC includes any story or piece of content created by a person about a brand or organisation that they share with their online networks.

The most obvious example of UGC is social media content, but it can also include product reviews, videos, blogs and many other formats and media. What these UGC forms have in common is that people use them as part of the research or decision-making process. UGC also shapes public opinion as it's seen as peer-to-peer information.

In the United States:

- 54% of adult Internet users regularly create and share photos and videos.

- Photos are also the most common form of UGC created by millennials.

- Product reviews make up 29% of UGC.

- The 25–34 (millennial) age group watches the most online videos.

When planning a government or public sector social media campaign, try to include an element that encourages UGC.

EXAMPLE: A government department focused on the environment has launched a new initiative to inform the public about the value of green spaces in their community. To spark conversation, inspiration and education, they launch a photo contest inviting citizens from across the country to share photos on Instagram of their favourite green space, tagging the photos with the hashtag #mygreenhome. The department is leveraging people power through social media, and having a national conversation with its citizens. The department complements their campaign with a video series with a YouTuber visiting some of the most scenic sights to bring them to life and to provide a live experience from the literal 'field'.

9. Identify influencers: establish who is influencing the conversation outside of your organisation

We're familiar with influencers who shape public debate: think about politicians, academics, authors, journalists and expert commentators. Influence in the Digital Age, or S3 Age (search, social and smart-phone), takes a different form, with often 'unknown' voices dominating public and online discourse. Online channels have allowed a new wave of influencers to take centre stage on many debates.

When a government agency seeks to influence and shape public opinion on a matter of public interest, they need to establish who is currently dominating the online conversations. By their very nature, they may already have built up a tribe of followers, who in turn become advocates for their messages.

There are numerous 'software as a service' (SaaS) platforms to help you identify the key influencers on any topic. Using algorithms and machine learning, these products can browse the social web and analyse trends and conversations, actions and interactions.

EXAMPLE: A government agency focused on international trade relations is hosting a conference on post-Brexit economic effects. They want to source influential speakers on a particular aspect of setting up new trade agreements. As part of their research, they set up a search query on a social listening platform for 'trilateral trade agreement concepts'. Very quickly, they identify key voices on Brexit, but also on the complementary subject of trilateral trade. The SaaS platform reinforces the influence of the individuals through their work being published in many media and journals.

10. Social listening: identify what citizens really
think and feel, in order to craft relevant messages

Calling in to radio shows or writing letters to the editor is how we used to have our voices heard. Now we have the value of being able to listen intently to the citizen voice on social media. Whether or not you agree with the concept of citizen journalism, we all have a voice and we can all influence public opinion.

Well-trained media spokespeople have their finger on the pulse of a nation, and can take the temperature around a particular topic. Government and public sector agencies should leverage publicly available big data to analyse public sentiment on matters of critical importance.

EXAMPLE: A public health agency has had to recall a generic drug following an investigation by the Food and Drug Administration (FDA). In an attempt to quickly allay public fears, the agency deploys social listening to assess the specific concerns of the public. The agency uses this information to populate a blog, prepare media statements, create social content and produce livestreams. When you communicate in the public interest, you must understand what the public care about. Social listening is how you can do this strategically and intentionally.

Situational analysis

Now that you understand how social media can be used to shape and influence public opinion, it is time to determine where you are on the influence barometer by doing a situational analysis.

Pick a campaign that is a priority within your department or organisation. Start with the traditional SWOT analysis, where you identify the strengths, weaknesses, opportunities and threats you face heading into this campaign.

I also suggest my own framework, Digital **NOW**, which stands for: **narrow** the digital audience, **own** the digital conversation, **win** the digital conversion.

The Digital NOW framework

1. Narrow the digital audience

Define challenge or opportunity

- What key message/s do you need the public to understand?

- Where are they on the Jefkins Transfer Process scale? What do you need to do to move them from one position to another?

Establish digital footprint

- What content exists online relating to this topic?

- Which voices are most influential?

- Where are people accessing the information? (From whom, and through what channels?)

- What level of influence do you have?

Define audience segment

- Gather audience demographic data, e.g., gender, age, location.

- Gather audience behaviour data, e.g., interests, device, social networks.

- Research audience keywords, i.e., words or phrases specific to the topic or idea you are promoting.

- Research influential social media accounts that your public follow or subscribe to, e.g., on Twitter, Instagram, Facebook, TikTok, LinkedIn, Snapchat, YouTube.

2. Own the digital conversation

Content research and planning

- Produce content that speaks to the public's interests or fears.

- Undertake keyword research using Google's keyword planner tool, Ahrefs or SEMrush.

- Undertake hashtag research on Keyhole or Hashtagify and within each social network.

- Use YouTube's own search function to establish top viewed videos based on specific keywords.

- Develop a content plan around the key topics you need to write about.

3. Win the digital conversion

Channels of choice
- Decide on your digital channels based on your research (audience and content).

Resources
- What is your budget for social ads and content creation?

- What team and talent are available to you?

- Do you need to outsource some elements?

- Can you involve other departments or teams?

Designing a social media campaign

When preparing a social media campaign, you must be clear on your audience, objectives and metrics. Don't wing a campaign—hope is not a strategy that will work on social media. Using a proven formula will set you up for success.

Setting your campaign objectives

In order to make an impact, you must be very clear on your campaign objectives. As a team, you must agree on these objectives before you hatch your plan. Here are some suggestions for how you can frame your mission:

- We want to have dominant social share of voice online on this topic.

- We want to change citizen behaviour. (Note: be prepared to explain how you will you measure this.)

- We want X citizens to take an action, signalling their intent and support to others, e.g., subscribe, download, register, view, share, like.

- We want the media narrative to shift to reflect our key messages.

- We want to launch a Facebook Group, web forum, an online tribe with X people engaged.

- We want this campaign to result in the public taking action on X with an X% penetration rate.

- We want to rank in the top three results on the first page of Google for X keywords/phrases.

- We want our website landing page to achieve X pageviews in X weeks.

Share your campaign objectives with the entire team. You should build out the campaign work plan by assigning key roles and individual objectives to each member of staff.

Here's an example of how this might work in practice:

- **Content manager:** Optimising all social and web content for Google, in line with keyword research.

- **Social media manager:** Building audiences and awareness in accordance with the audience research phase, and monitoring conversations around the topic.

- **Website manager:** Ensuring speed, user experience and optimisation of landing page.

- **Performance manager:** Optimising advertising campaigns by using A/B testing and reviewing funnel analytics.

Top Tip

CAMPAIGNS SHOULD HAVE one dedicated landing page that has no distractions and that provides as much information as possible. Depending on the nature of the topic, you may need supplementary pages, but the initial landing page must be engaging, optimised and have relevant content.

Social media campaign blueprint

Here are the fundamental steps to follow when building your next social media campaign:

1. Set the **campaign timeframe**, i.e., start date and end date (even if over a long period of time).

2. List your key overall **campaign goals.**
   - Include **milestone goals** within the campaign timeframe to establish what you need to achieve and by when.

3. Document three to five **key pillar messages** you will share during the campaign that will bind it together.

4. Agree on a branded **hashtag** for the campaign that will be associated with your organisation.
   - Make it unique, campaign-specific and topic-based.
   - Use research to find **relevant trending hashtags** that can complement your campaign and generate discoverability.
   - Use topic hashtags frequently.

5. Select the **digital content formats** and assets you will create for this campaign:

☐ Facebook Live
☐ Twitter Live
☐ Instagram Live
☐ Instagram Stories
☐ Instagram Reels
☐ TikTok video
☐ YouTube vlog/interview/piece to camera
☐ Facebook native video (20 seconds)
☐ Facebook Stories
☐ Twitter native video (30 seconds)
☐ Twitter Space
☐ LinkedIn video (45 seconds)
☐ Blog posts (list headlines for each)
☐ Email marketing (list the subject lines for each email sequence)
☐ Landing page (include the URL, e.g., organisation.com/ campaign name)
☐ Quote graphics
☐ Audiograms (audio with an image overlay to create a social video)
☐ Webinar
☐ White paper
☐ E-book
☐ Guide
☐ FAQ
☐ Live website chat
☐ Podcast episode
☐ Facebook Group
☐ Twitter Chat
☐ LinkedIn article
☐ Medium article
☐ Podcast (guest on podcasts or create your own series)

6. Define your **calls to action.**
   - Be clear on what you want your audience to do. It can be more than one action.

7. List the **channels** you are going to use:
   - [ ] Website
   - [ ] Social media
   - [ ] Podcast
   - [ ] Email
   - [ ] PPC (pay per click) ads
   - [ ] Forum
   - [ ] Intranet
   - [ ] Other

8. Choose the **face and voice** of your campaign.
   - This person should be a subject matter expert, have authority and be in the know with all the necessary information.
   - In addition to staff members, you may also include expert spokespersons, citizens, case studies and testimonials, influencers or celebrities.

9. Use a **stepped approach** to gain momentum, i.e., awareness, engagement and conversion.
   - List which of the pillar messages from step three you will push out during the three phases of your campaign. You can change the timeframe based on your unique campaign duration.

STEPPED CAMPAIGN TIMING FRAMEWORK

TIMEFRAME	OBJECTIVE	MESSAGE
Weeks 1–3	Awareness	
Weeks 4–6	Engagement	
Weeks 7–8	Conversion	

10. Determine which **social media tactics** you will follow, for which platform:

Facebook
- ☐ Paid posts using targeted advertising
- ☐ Promoted videos
- ☐ Re-marketing based on video views/landing pageviews
- ☐ Facebook Livestream
- ☐ Native video
- ☐ Facebook Group
- ☐ Building saved audiences in Facebook Ads Manager

Twitter
- ☐ Hashtag/s
- ☐ Twitter Chat
- ☐ Native video
- ☐ Twitter Live
- ☐ Lists (capturing influential voices and accounts)
- ☐ Promoted Tweets

LinkedIn
- ☐ Status updates
- ☐ Article
- ☐ Native video
- ☐ Live video
- ☐ Hashtags
- ☐ LinkedIn sponsored content
- ☐ LinkedIn sponsored InMail

YouTube
- ☐ Episodic series (playlist)
- ☐ YouTube Live
- ☐ Collaboration with influencer

11. Determine the types of **social media advertising** you'll create, and your budget, for which platform:

   ☐ Facebook
   ☐ Instagram
   ☐ Twitter
   ☐ Snapchat
   ☐ LinkedIn
   ☐ YouTube
   ☐ TikTok

12. Finally, consider ways to encourage **user-generated content (UGC)** among the public, using a variety of formats that include:

   ☐ Contest/s
   ☐ Hashtag
   ☐ Influencer collaboration
   ☐ Media partnership

Measuring campaign success

A metric is a quantifiable measure of one specific piece of data. When you measure campaign success, you must first align the metrics against your original objectives. You can read more about metrics and how you can use them in chapter 11, but here are just a few examples of metrics you might measure for a specific campaign:

Website
☐ Unique sessions
☐ Conversions/goals, e.g., downloads, subscriptions, event registrations
☐ Time on landing page
☐ Pageviews (blogs, landing pages)
☐ Audience data, i.e., gender, age, location, device
☐ Referral traffic source using UTM tracking

Facebook

☐ Fan growth (during campaign phase)
☐ Reach
☐ Engagement
☐ Top Facebook post
☐ Top video
☐ Share of voice
☐ Sentiment
☐ Profile of audience engaged (Facebook Ads)
☐ Video views
☐ Video retention rate
☐ Relevance score (Facebook Ads)
☐ Click-through rate (Facebook Ads)
☐ Cost per lead (Facebook Ads)
☐ Website traffic generated

Twitter

☐ Follower growth (during campaign phase)
☐ Reach/impressions
☐ Profile visits
☐ Engagement
☐ Favourites
☐ ReTweets
☐ Top Tweet
☐ Total video views
☐ Top follower
☐ Share of voice
☐ Sentiment
☐ Website traffic generated

Instagram

☐ Follower growth (during campaign phase)
☐ Reach
☐ Engagement
☐ Top post
☐ Instagram Stories reach

- [ ] Instagram Stories engagement
- [ ] Instagram Stories views
- [ ] Instagram Stories swipe-ups
- [ ] Website traffic generated

LinkedIn

Note: I recommend that a senior leader who is the voice of the campaign leverages their personal LinkedIn profile to share key messages on the platform.

- [ ] Follower/connections growth (during campaign phase)
- [ ] Reach
- [ ] Engagement
- [ ] Top status update
- [ ] Article engagement (views, likes, comments, shares)
- [ ] Total video views

YouTube

- [ ] Subscriber growth (during campaign phase)
- [ ] Total video views
- [ ] Video engagement (likes, comments, shares)
- [ ] Top video
- [ ] Website referral traffic

TikTok

- [ ] Video views
- [ ] New followers
- [ ] Engagement rate

Hashtag (across platforms)

- [ ] Reach
- [ ] Impressions
- [ ] Engagement
- [ ] Top influencers
- [ ] Top accounts
- [ ] Trends (if it trended, where and when)

Email marketing

- ☐ Email open rate
- ☐ Link click-through rate
- ☐ Conversion rate
- ☐ Bounce rate
- ☐ List growth rate
- ☐ Email sharing/forwarding rate

Online media mentions

- ☐ Mentions on media websites
- ☐ Domain authority score
- ☐ Traffic generated from online media mentions
- ☐ Online mentions from media social networks
- ☐ Reach from mentions on media social networks
- ☐ Number of backlinks from media websites
- ☐ Podcast interviews
- ☐ Podcast show downloads
- ☐ Video interviews
- ☐ Video views

SEO (keyword-specific)

- ☐ Keywords ranking (Google, Bing, Yahoo!, etc.)
- ☐ Organic traffic
- ☐ Click-through rate
- ☐ Domain authority
- ☐ Page speed

Top Tip

CHECK YOUR DOMAIN authority using the **Website Authority Checker** tool at seoreviewtools.com/website-authority-checker, and use **Ahrefs Backlink Checker** (ahrefs.com/backlink-checker) to establish which prominent sites are backlinking to your site. By monitoring the number of incoming links and referring domains your website has, you can assess the impact on your website's SEO. Every link you earn has the potential to improve your domain authority, and links from new domains will almost always have a bigger impact than links from sites that already link to you. You can also use **Google's PageSpeed Insights tool** (developers.google .com/speed/pagespeed/insights) to see how fast your website is—speed is one of the biggest factors in creating a good user experience.

There is no doubt that social media can inspire citizens to take action when they trust the government agency telling the story. However, a lack of consistent and defined messaging will have the opposite effect.

WHEN FACED WITH A communications challenge, embrace social media and let it do the digital legwork for you. Be clear on your message, be clear on the citizen grouping you want to speak to and be vociferous in your consistent messaging. Don't forget to use video as your storytelling ally and be brave enough to go front of screen. You will learn more about appropriate video creation in chapter 7.

How to Develop a Social Media Strategy for Government or a Public Sector Agency

Leveraging the power of social networks to engage citizens

Social media for government agencies, unlike social media for businesses, isn't focused largely on making sales. There are, of course, some government agencies that have to meet revenue goals or sales targets, such as economic development agencies whose role it is to attract foreign direct investment, or a museum that must ensure it is financially self-sufficient. But the public interest message that you are communicating is going to be the hook to get your ideal audience to sit up, listen and ultimately take action.

Your work is entirely geared towards creating an environment of communication. No matter what role you have in a public sector body, your success will be based on the strength of the communications surrounding your project, plan or campaign. With this in mind, you need to build trust, be transparent and provide timely customer service that will let citizens in your area know that you are working for them, while also encouraging them to respond to your calls to action.

In this chapter, we'll cover the social media landscape, setting 12-month social media goals, the tone you should be using in your communications and the attributes of an outstanding social media community manager.

The social media global landscape

In 10 years, to 2021, there has been a 217% increase in social media use, and in 12 months, to 2022, there has been double-digit growth (10%). Social media use is showing no signs of slowing, but many signs of evolving. With 12.5 trillion hours spent online, representing a new milestone in Internet adoption, and new records for social media use, we are knocking on the door of the Engagement Age, where every touchpoint available to citizens is driven by their personal need, and not by how government and public sector want to push, publish and broadcast.

If you thought we would return to normal in 2022, from a communications perspective, then you were misguided. In this chapter, we are going to recalibrate and reimagine our own communications approach—from a place of citizen engagement, not organisation need.

We must first establish the social media landscape and the change in citizen behaviour on these channels.

There are three core requirements for successful strategic social media:

1. Capability
2. Capacity
3. Consistency

Capability: the skills required to maximise the trends on each channel.

Capacity: time and resources prioritised for social media output.

Consistency: showing up for your audience on time, every time.

You don't need to be everywhere! Let's take some time to consider the types of audiences using each social network, and the factors you should consider when deciding which to focus on and grow.

Constant advancements in technology have led to many individual changes in behaviour that accumulate into larger trends. I need think no further than my children: Sophie is 27 and Bobby is 13, and that 14-year gap provides invaluable insights for me as a digital marketer.

The social media playing field keeps changing. TikTok is eating into the Meta monopoly; Facebook and Instagram are now responding to TikTok trends; social messaging is mainstream; citizens expect Twitter, WhatsApp and Messenger to be used as social customer service channels; and YouTube continues to own social search as a long-form video platform. Meanwhile social audio is becoming the new tactic on the social media block and is growing in relevance following in the footsteps of the podcasting boom.

The TikTok takeover

TikTok's evolution from a lip-syncing, dance-dueting, kid-beloved app to an adult education, entertainment and encyclopaedia of all-types-of-everything social network has disrupted social media since the first edition of this book was published.

The appeal centres on it being video-first, full-screen mobile immersive; fronted by humans engaged in storytelling and sharing insights, hacks and diary entries; overlaid with popular music, trendy transitions and special effects, thus satisfying the masses with a feast for the visual, aural and egotistical senses.

Social Media Network Usage and Trends

OF THE GLOBAL POPULATION, 58% are active social media users. When we look at the global population aged 13+ using social media this percentage jumps to 75%.

Social media leaderboard

Looking to the social networks with most monthly active users (MAU), the 2022 figures, at time of writing, are:
- Facebook: 2.9 billion
- YouTube: 2.6 billion
- WhatsApp: 2 billion
- Instagram: 1.5 billion
- WeChat: 1.3 billion
- TikTok: 1 billion
- Facebook Messenger: 990 million
- LinkedIn: 740 million registered users/ 55 million registered companies
- Snapchat: 560 million
- Twitter: 436 million
- Reddit: 430 million

Time spent online
- The average time spent daily using social media is 2 hours and 27 minutes
- The average time spent daily listening to podcasts is 55 minutes

Watching online video content
- 92% of Internet users watch video online weekly
- 51% watch music videos
- 37% watch viral/meme videos
- 31% watch how-to/tutorial videos
- 30% watch livestreams
- 30% watch educational videos
- 28% watch product review videos

- 29% watch sports clips or highlights videos
- 27% watch gaming videos
- 27% watch influencer videos and vlogs

Social marketing stats worth noting

- 85% of marketers ranked short-form videos as the most effective type of social media content in 2021.

- 1.3 million new users joined social media every day in 2020.

- Millennials are logged on to social media for an average of 2 hours and 38 minutes daily, while Gen Z logs on for 2 hours and 55 minutes daily.

- Political content is the most viewed genre on Facebook Stories.

- The average TikTok user will spend 52 minutes a day on the platform, or 26 hours and 52 minutes per month.

- Life hacks and general advice is the ninth most popular content type on TikTok with 8 billion video views.

- 55% of TikTok users are publishing TikTok videos.

- Link clicks account for 92% of all user interaction with Tweets.

- Tweets with hashtags get 100% more engagement.

- 64% of Instagram users are under the age of 34.

- 98% of marketers say Instagram is the most influential platform for influencer marketing, which is 44% higher than Facebook.

- 60% of LinkedIn users are between 25 and 34 years old.

- Over 46% of all social media traffic to company websites comes from LinkedIn.

- The number of YouTube users is projected to reach 2.8 million by 2025.

Sources: Twitter, Facebook, HubSpot, World Economic Forum, Global-WebIndex, Sprout Social, Statista, DataReportal

Setting 12-month social media goals

Before ramping up your social media outputs, take a step back. Ask yourself what social media return on investment (ROI) you need to deliver for your organisation. There are many key areas to focus on as you build your social media marketing strategy. Understanding those areas and establishing clear goals is critical to building a social media platform that is geared towards providing the information necessary for visitors.

When setting your social media goals, you must be fully aware of the overall communications objectives of your department or organisation. If you are not aware, get briefed on them. Your social media strategy should complement and support these objectives.

Here are some broad objectives that you might identify with:

- Providing customer service (with defined timeframes).
- Sharing real-time alerts and public interest messages.
- Emergency response management.
- Increased awareness around specific public interest campaigns.
- Building trust.
- Displaying transparency.
- Introducing and showcasing your people.
- Providing a voice for senior leadership.
- Correcting the record and counteracting fake news.
- Encouraging the public to take a specific action to support behavioural change.
- Digital PR and media engagement.
- Reputation management (organisational and individual).
- Sharing expert knowledge and insights.
- Promoting public interest campaigns linked to public policy.
- Driving website traffic.
- Increasing your social media community.
- Increasing community reach and engagement.
- Building a community of advocates for particular public interest campaigns.

Here are some examples of goals with linked key performance indicators that you might set in your social media strategy:

- 'Social media will be responsible for 20% of all of our web traffic in the next 12 months.'

- 'In six months, we will have all our senior leaders on Twitter delivering core corporate messages with a personal touch.'

- 'We will grow our Instagram community by 15% in 12 months with an average engagement rate of 2% (newsfeed and Stories).'

- 'We will publish education messages linked to key campaigns on TikTok growing our account targeting 18–25-year-olds.'

- 'Staff will be offered training on LinkedIn with a view to rolling out a staff social advocacy programme with 40% of staff in the senior leadership team active weekly by year-end.'

Conducting a social media audit

As a government or public sector agency, keeping the public informed is a critical part of your social media strategy. Consistency of publishing and the relevance of your messaging is central to building and maintaining trust and transparency for your organisation. To begin creating your social media strategy, start by auditing your existing social networks and assessing how well they are performing for you, and how well you are adhering to the best practices for each platform.

Initial social media audit guide

Twitter
Twitter profile set-up checklist:

- ☐ Audience profile defined
- ☐ Moderation policy defined
- ☐ Full organisation/department/individual name
- ☐ Branded Twitter handle: @username

- ☐ Engaging, 160-character bio complete
- ☐ Bio uses keyword-rich descriptions
- ☐ Branded/campaign hashtag used
- ☐ Website/landing page link in bio
- ☐ Email address for public in bio
- ☐ Twitter moderation policy outlined
- ☐ Twitter abuse policy outlined
- ☐ Location listed (where appropriate)
- ☐ Away-from-Twitter customer service email contact posted
- ☐ Optimised profile photo (400px by 400px) reflects you/organisation
- ☐ Optimised header photo (1500px by 500px) with tagline
- ☐ Pinned Tweet with call to action (CTA)
- ☐ Colour theme matches branding
- ☐ Categorised Twitter lists for social listening
- ☐ Featured Moment to showcase your story
- ☐ Safe login password saved on file
- ☐ Following 10 new users per day based on keyword research and engagement
- ☐ Monitoring 1:1 following/follower ratio
- ☐ Quarterly audience analysis: are our followers reflective of our target audiences on Twitter?

Twitter posting checklist:

- ☐ Posting 2–6 times daily
- ☐ Adding value to your followers
- ☐ Content shared matches brand ethos
- ☐ Tweets in brand voice
- ☐ Using 1–2 hashtags in each Tweet, especially branded/trending
- ☐ Each Tweet is relevant and has value
- ☐ Posting a diverse mix of videos, images, links and text posts
- ☐ Monthly analytics report created
- ☐ Monthly hashtag report created
- ☐ Twice-yearly audit of fake followers/non-engaged users and delete
- ☐ Responding to comments and engaging followers
- ☐ Managing spam

- [ ] Adding followers to lists
- [ ] Sending traffic to relevant landing pages
- [ ] Quote-Tweeting others
- [ ] Hours of activity on Twitter logged
- [ ] Two-factor authentication turned on

Facebook Page

Facebook Page set-up checklist:

- [ ] Audience defined
- [ ] Moderation policy defined
- [ ] Confirm page is a Facebook Page and not a profile for department/organisation/public figure
- [ ] Review category of Page
- [ ] Customised @username URL (5–50 characters)
- [ ] Organisation/department/public figure name used (70 characters)
- [ ] 'About' section completed (155 characters)
- [ ] Website/landing page URL added
- [ ] Optimised and quality profile photo (logo/headshot, 180px by 180px; note: will display 160px by 160px on desktop or 140px by 140px on smartphones)
- [ ] Optimised cover photo (399px by 150px; note: will display 851px by 315px on desktop or 640px by 360px on smartphones)
- [ ] Page accessed via approved personal profiles (not a fake profile)
- [ ] 2+ admins (one must be a department manager)
- [ ] Status of admins reviewed (admin, editor, advertiser, analyst)
- [ ] Business Instagram account connected
- [ ] Facebook Group linked to Page
- [ ] Story section complete
- [ ] Image descriptions completed
- [ ] Call to action button selected
- [ ] Moderation policy and fan guidelines in long description
- [ ] Facebook abuse policy outlined
- [ ] Privacy settings optimised
- [ ] Business Manager set up and accounts, admins and agency linked
- [ ] Facebook Protect activated with two-factor authentication turned on

Facebook Page posting checklist:

- ☐ Post once daily
- ☐ Weekly video
- ☐ Monthly livestream
- ☐ Tag in posts where relevant
- ☐ Review insights monthly for best times of day to post
- ☐ Diverse mix of image, video, link, text, live posts
- ☐ Review insights to establish which of above get most engagement
- ☐ Mix of content themes
- ☐ Curate third-party content with comment
- ☐ Engage with fans (emoticons and text response)
- ☐ Share relevant content to Page Story
- ☐ Share relevant content from Instagram to Page
- ☐ Add milestones
- ☐ Regularly update cover photo and include a status update to give context

Facebook Group

Facebook Group set-up checklist:

- ☐ Audience defined
- ☐ Moderation policy defined
- ☐ Abuse policy posted
- ☐ Activity calendar created
- ☐ Name of Group reflects audience and goals
- ☐ Review Group category/type
- ☐ Privacy settings (public/closed/secret) correct
- ☐ Optimised cover photo (851px by 315px for desktop or 640px by 360px for smartphone)
- ☐ Icon to Group reviewed/added
- ☐ 2+ admins on the Group
- ☐ Member questions set up (to vet Group members)
- ☐ Group location reviewed
- ☐ Set up Learning Units (if relevant)
- ☐ Members reviewed

Facebook Group posting checklist:

☐ Tags reviewed
☐ Scheduled posts
☐ Review Group insights monthly
☐ Engage with all members
☐ Ask questions to admit members and get agreement to Group rules
☐ Welcome post for new members
☐ Welcome new members as they arrive
☐ Regular live video into Group
☐ Host a regular livestream or Q&A session
☐ Add or remove members as necessary
☐ Moderate content in keeping with Group ethos and rules

LinkedIn Company Page

LinkedIn company page profile set-up checklist:

☐ Audience defined
☐ Moderation policy defined
☐ Organisation/department name used (100 characters)
☐ Pinned post (24/7)
☐ Correct website/landing page URL
☐ Set up showcase pages with keyword-rich descriptions
☐ 2+ admins, including a manager
☐ Review status of admins (designated admin, direct sponsored, content poster, recruiting poster) and admin rights
☐ Review header image
☐ Completed keyword-rich description (200–2,000 characters)
☐ Address current
☐ URL customised
☐ Staff invited to follow page

LinkedIn company page posting checklist:

☐ Posting checklist created
☐ Engage with followers

- ☐ Daily company update
- ☐ Curate posts with comments
- ☐ Captions for images always (150 characters)
- ☐ Content aligned to audiences needs
- ☐ Vanity URLs on posts (bit.ly)
- ☐ Branded imagery on posts
- ☐ Optimised post images (1200px by 627px)
- ☐ CTA on posts, or post a question
- ☐ Use relevant hashtags
- ☐ Review language-specific information (name, description)
- ☐ Use tracking links
- ☐ Use sponsored content options
- ☐ Target updates to specific audiences (where relevant)
- ☐ Share a variety of content types: link posts, image, video, text-based
- ☐ Creative content mix, including how-to, opinion, seasonal, themed, industry or topical
- ☐ Consideration of live video and rules of engagement for staff in setting up a live broadcast
- ☐ Opinion/expert-led intro content on posts
- ☐ 4-1-1 rule (post 4 pieces of new curated content, 1 repost and 1 self-promotion post)
- ☐ Review analytics monthly

Personal LinkedIn Profile

LinkedIn personal profile set-up checklist:

- ☐ Audience defined
- ☐ Full name used (former names can be included in brackets so long-time colleagues can find you) and pronouns defined
- ☐ Recent high-quality headshot used
- ☐ Professional headline, with 120 characters describing precisely your expertise
- ☐ Job title and organisation/s you work for included
- ☐ Limited or no use of obscure acronyms
- ☐ Work and geographic location settings optimised
- ☐ Profile summary complete (2,000 characters)

- [ ] Current and past positions; at least three skills included
- [ ] Visual media used, e.g., past work, infographics or career high-light videos
- [ ] Past awards, volunteer experience and association membership included
- [ ] Professional headline optimised
- [ ] URL personalised
- [ ] Turn on Creator Mode: add five industry keywords to highlight your particular expertise
- [ ] At least three recommendations gathered
- [ ] As much contact information as you are comfortable with posting

LinkedIn personal profile posting checklist:

- [ ] Three updates weekly
- [ ] Share original content
- [ ] Curate articles with added comment
- [ ] Engage regularly with likes, comments, shares
- [ ] Download mobile app
- [ ] Connect with 10 new people weekly
- [ ] Manage endorsements and connection requests (do not ignore)
- [ ] Seek and give endorsements
- [ ] Seek and give recommendations
- [ ] Connect with past and current work colleagues
- [ ] Expand network by finding people in your organisation, industry and with similar skillsets
- [ ] Add new and relevant sections to your profile, e.g., volunteering, awards, certifications
- [ ] Include media (e.g., photos, graphics, web links, video)
- [ ] Use relevant hashtags

Instagram

Instagram profile set-up checklist:

- [ ] Audience defined
- [ ] Moderation policy defined
- [ ] Account name correct and reflective of organisation/department

- ☐ Confirm profile is business account
- ☐ Bio complete, and speaks to ideal audience
- ☐ Hashtags and emojis used to optimise 150 characters
- ☐ Link in bio, updated for current campaign
- ☐ 2+ people with access, including a manager
- ☐ Location on, if relevant
- ☐ Instagram account connected to Facebook Page
- ☐ Storyboards created for Stories
- ☐ Stories content plan in place

Instagram posting checklist:

- ☐ Post once daily
- ☐ Content makes sense for audience
- ☐ Content makes sense for organisation's brand
- ☐ Content is not offensive or easily misinterpreted
- ☐ Timing is optimal
- ☐ Use best hashtags for campaign
- ☐ Use branded and/or campaign hashtags
- ☐ Responding to comments and engaging with community
- ☐ Captions are engaging
- ☐ Content fits well in the Instagram grid

YouTube

YouTube profile set-up checklist:

- ☐ Audience defined
- ☐ Moderation policy defined
- ☐ Username reflective of organisation/department
- ☐ Account connected to organisation's Google account/Gmail address
- ☐ URL is customised
- ☐ Review list of password holders
- ☐ Review strength of password
- ☐ 2+ people with access, including a manager
- ☐ 'About' section complete with 1,000-character profile, channel country, business email and links
- ☐ Channel profile icon optimised (800px by 800px)

☐ Channel art (cover image) complete (image size 2560px by 1440px, with logo and text within central 'safe area' of 1546px by 423px)
☐ Titles (100 characters) and descriptions (4,850 characters) unique and optimised with keywords and URLs
☐ Video playlists created
☐ Explanatory channel trailer created for unsubscribed visitors

YouTube posting checklist:

☐ Frequency dependent on organisation's strategy
☐ At least one monthly vlog
☐ YouTube Live being used
☐ CTA and request to subscribe in each video
☐ Videos fully optimised
☐ Tags added to videos (500 characters)
☐ Branded YouTube thumbnails for each video
☐ Videos embedded in blog posts

Google My Business

GMB profile checklist:

☐ Audience defined
☐ Account claimed and verified
☐ Profile information complete and up to date
☐ URL customised
☐ Username is correct
☐ Review list of password holders
☐ Review strength of password
☐ 2+ people with access, including a manager
☐ Organisation's URL listed
☐ Tagline is descriptive (optimal 40 characters)
☐ 'About' section complete (3,000 characters)
☐ Contact information included
☐ Profile picture optimised (750px by 750px) and reflects organisation
☐ Cover photo optimised (1080px by 608px) and reflects organisation

TikTok

TikTok profile set-up checklist:

☐ Audience defined
☐ Moderation policy defined
☐ 80-character bio drafted to include keywords and hashtag/s
☐ Set to business profile status
☐ Upload profile photo (logo)
☐ Choose username
☐ Add website link
☐ Connect your other social networks
☐ Get your account verified
☐ Review privacy settings

TikTok posting checklist:

☐ 100 characters max for caption
☐ Trending hashtags included in caption including For You Page (hashtag #fyp)
☐ 2–3 videos per week
☐ Batch produce videos and save for regular posting
☐ Share TikTok video to Stories
☐ Add trending sound on TikTok video
☐ Lean into trends for content ideation
☐ Add bold headline text to grab users' attention
☐ Add call to action in your video (e.g., follow for more videos like this)
☐ Allow Duets on your videos
☐ Allow Stitching on your videos

Snapchat

Snapchat profile set-up checklist:

☐ Audience defined
☐ Moderation policy defined
☐ Username is reflective of our organisation/department
☐ Snapcode/username shared on other social networks

- ☐ Spam or abusive accounts blocked
- ☐ 2+ people with access, including a manager
- ☐ Insights reviewed regularly

Snapchat posting checklist:

- ☐ Stories content plan created
- ☐ Storyboards created for each story
- ☐ Daily Snaps posted
- ☐ Tone of voice is appropriate
- ☐ Focus on themes
- ☐ Snaps from audience responded to quickly
- ☐ Pillar Stories weekly (focusing on one key issue)
- ☐ Snaps are creative and use all available features

Pinterest

Pinterest profile set-up checklist:

- ☐ Audience defined
- ☐ Moderation policy defined
- ☐ Username is reflective of organisation/department
- ☐ URL customised
- ☐ 2+ admins, including a manager
- ☐ Bio completed (160 characters)
- ☐ Website URL included in bio
- ☐ Profile image optimised (165px by 165px)
- ☐ Pinned images used
- ☐ Website has Pinterest widget for users

Pinterest posting checklist:

- ☐ All blog posts shared
- ☐ All YouTube videos shared
- ☐ All important speeches or press releases shared
- ☐ Relevant boards followed
- ☐ Existing content examined for possible repurpose

WhatsApp

WhatsApp profile set-up checklist:

- ☐ Audience defined
- ☐ Moderation policy defined
- ☐ WhatsApp Groups being used
- ☐ Purpose and guidelines made clear to members
- ☐ 2+ admins on all groups, including a manager

WhatsApp posting checklist:

- ☐ Posting in accordance with need
- ☐ Monitoring messages regularly, with quick response

CASE STUDY: Who Owns Our Social Networks— Staff or the Organisation?

A LEGAL CASE involving a US newspaper shows the importance of strong passwords and ownership policies, and of rescinding passwords when an employee leaves the organisation. The *Roanoke Times* in Virginia sued a former employee when he refused to hand over the logins to the publication's Twitter account in a case challenging ownership rights. The newspaper had clearly set out in its employee handbook that employees who have been issued 'company-owned information assets, keys or other access items must return them to the company upon termination of employment.' However, the official Twitter account was in the control of sports reporter Andy Bitter, who left to join a rival title using said Twitter account to leverage his profile. When the newspaper sued for loss of a company asset, Bitter countersued for defamation. Both parties ended up settling out of court; however, there's no doubt it left a bitter taste in the mouth of the newspaper who failed to lock down ownership rights on social networks.

Channels, content and frequency

One of my most frequently asked questions is: 'How often should I post on X social network?' The answer is contained in these three key points:

1. Posting *consistency* is more important than posting *frequency*.

2. Content *quality* is more important than content *quantity* (and social networks are letting us know this with ongoing algorithm changes).

3. Without having an *objective* for social media, you won't know if your posts are successful or not.

Creating a posting schedule

Like any other entity, you need a solid posting schedule to help ensure that your social media pages remain active and engaging. Citizens don't want to follow government agencies that rarely provide them with the information they need, and a failure to provide that information can lead to a lack of trust or concerns over transparency.

Make sure that your social media posting schedule includes the following considerations:

1. *Government communications standards*

Depending on your department, there may be times of the year when you need to communicate more frequently with your followers in order to provide them with the information they need. Your local department of education, for example, may need to offer more posts at the start or end of the school year, while the local park service may need to provide more frequent posts during the spring or autumn.

2. *Regular posting plans*

Will you post daily? Weekly? How often do citizens really want to hear from your office? Take into consideration how much awareness you think citizens currently have of your office and what it is able to accomplish, then decide how much more often you need to communicate with your citizens in order to provide them with better standards of information.

3. Disaster plans

During a disaster, your regular plans frequently go out the window. However, you don't want to overwhelm newsfeeds with irrelevant information or updates that do not genuinely provide any benefit. Consider how often it is appropriate to post during a disaster—and how often you should check in with your followers, even if it is just to reassure them that nothing has changed.

You can monitor your social channel insights, which will tell you when you get most engagement. For those of you who want extra guidance, here is a general rule for each social network:

Facebook: 1–2 posts per day

Why? If you have fewer than 10,000 followers, you should post one or fewer times per day. Once you exceed one post, each post gets 60% fewer clicks per post. If you have more than 10,000 followers, posting 1–2 times per day leads to the most clicks per post.

YouTube: 1 video per week

Why? Consistent posting of videos will result in views. By having a weekly video/show, you are telling your audience that you will have a regular schedule, and thus they have a reason to tune in.

Instagram: 1–2 posts per day

Why? The 55 top-performing brands on Instagram post, on average, 1.5 times per day.

Instagram Stories: 3–4 stories per week

Why? You want to build up a captive audience, so consistency is really important. If you are inconsistent, you will not build up loyalty.

Twitter: 3–5 Tweets per day

Why? In a study by Socialbakers, brands that Tweeted 2–5 times per day had the highest response rate. If brands only Tweeted once a day, there was a 300% difference in response rate, and response per Tweet started dropping off after 5 times per day. A sample of 11,000 Tweets from top brands showed brands see their most engagement when Tweeting 3 times per day; that engagement begins dropping after 3 Tweets per day.

TikTok: 1 video per week to start building up to 3 per week

Why? When you post regularly on TikTok you are rewarded by extra exposure and returning video viewers.

LinkedIn: 1 post per day

Why? When you post 20 times per month (or one post per day during the work week), you'll reach at least 60% of your audience.

Pinterest: 3 Pins per day

Why? A study of top consumer brands found most were Pinning anywhere from a few times a week to 3–10 times per day. A noticeable number of brands were Pinning in excess of 10 times per day; however, fewer of those brands were experiencing rapid growth, so it is safe to assume it is best to Pin 3 or more times per day on Pinterest.

Snapchat: 2–5 Snaps per day

Why? If you want to build an engaged audience, you have to show up regularly. Snapchat is an easy-to-use platform and you can Snap on the go, but consider your topic and story.

A social media strategy with culture in mind

It is important to build a culture of citizen-first engagement into your social media strategy, otherwise you will be doing social media for social media's sake. What follows are a few cultural issues you should keep in mind in building your social media strategy.

1. Trust and transparency

As you are working to establish trust and transparency, you will need to create an environment that can be trustworthy. Examine your social media accounts for these elements:

- Are you providing accurate, honest information to the best of your ability?

- Are you willing to make things right when you've made a mistake, whether it is failing to share information or sharing it inaccurately?

- Do you have an open policy about information sharing, or are you preventing people from posting about specific information on your social networks?

2. Ownership

Note also that ownership is very important when it comes to social networks. When senior leaders or staff members are setting up accounts for your organisation or department, it must be clear who owns the account. A good rule of thumb:

- Account connected to role in organisation: belongs to organisation (e.g., @POTUS).

- Account set up with your own credentials but mentions your job in the bio: belongs to individual (e.g., @JoeBiden).

3. Customer service

When building out a customer service policy, you need to ask yourself some fundamental questions, such as: What type of service do our social media fans and followers need from us? And on what channels will we provide it? Furthermore, there are several key elements that your office will need to address in order to create effective customer service through your social networks. These include questions like:

- What information do our fans genuinely need? This includes both the latest updates and information pertaining to current emergencies.

- Are we providing open communication with our fans and followers, including answers to their questions and the opportunity for them to discuss current issues?

- Do our fans and followers know that they can turn to us to help them when there is a problem?

4. Citizens taking action

One of your key social media goals may be to encourage citizens to take action. They might need to vote on a specific issue (or vote to keep you in office), increase awareness about public health concerns or attend a specific local event. Are your social networks encouraging citizens to take action? Do your citizens:

- Share the information you have posted?
- Attend the events you have shared with them?
- Get involved in local community outreach as a result of information on your page?

The metrics you need to track your social media culture

While it may be difficult to calculate 'citizen satisfaction', using the right metrics can help ensure that you are connecting more effectively with citizens who are impacted by your department. These metrics include:

- How many fans or followers does your page have? (The right number depends on your platform.)

- Are your fans and followers increasing or decreasing over time? If you have seen a sudden increase in fans, consider why. If there has been a recent decrease, it is time to check your current popularity ratings and response to your posts in order to understand the trend.

- How many likes and shares do your posts receive across your platforms? Are you creating information that your citizens are eager to share, or are you simply posting boring information that they scroll past?

- How engaging are your posts? What types of posts are most likely to encourage commentary from people who see it? How does what you post influence your fans and followers?

Establishing a consistent tone of voice

One of the critical parts of designing a social media strategy is establishing your voice. This is true both of businesses and the public sector, or anyone who wants to build their social media presence. Visitors to your page want consistency. They want to know that they can trust your page to provide them with consistently accurate information, and they want to have the same experience with your office no matter where they may be dealing with you. On social media, that means establishing a clear voice and guidelines for posting that will be used by anyone who posts through your social media account.

Your tone of voice should reflect your core values. Here are some examples:

- Promote (e.g., health and safety messages)
- Research (e.g., science)
- Advise (e.g., political party)
- Partner (e.g., other public sector bodies to promote a shared message)
- Independent (e.g., we are independent of government views)
- Expert (e.g., we know what we are talking about and are a go-to resource)
- Trustworthy (e.g., you can trust what we say and what we do)

Who will be the 'face' of your account?

As a public sector or government organisation, you may have a specific face that you want to put in front of your social media campaign. You want citizens to recognise you and support your work. Government agencies, like local municipal authorities and police departments, might choose either to speak with a single voice ('we believe...', 'we wish to inform...') or to establish specific personalities for individuals who are able to post on the account. You may also choose to use a staff member who essentially becomes your social media reporter.

How do you want to communicate?

As a government agency, you want to provide serious, accurate information to your social media users, but that doesn't mean you are stuck with a dry, boring tone. You might, for example, decide that you want to create a humorous presence on social media, regularly posting jokes that appeal to your fans. As you design your presence, carefully consider the education level and other attributes of the people who are most likely to engage with your social media accounts for regular information. The Flesch guide to readability suggests that what we write online should be able to be read by an 11-year-old. Your tone of voice should be reflective of the level of emotional connection the public has with you.

Know when to drop the voice

During an emergency such as a flood, tornado or terrorist attack, it is okay to drop whatever voice you have created and post serious content that is respectful of the disaster. You can always return to your regularly scheduled posts when the disaster has passed. Be sure to delete scheduled posts during a crisis, as it is likely they will jar sitting with more serious and real-time breaking news.

THE TONE OF VOICE MATRIX

TONE OF VOICE	HOW TO DISPLAY IT ONLINE
Helpful	'Did you know?' content
Friendly	Faces of our organisation need to be visible, e.g., weekly Facebook Q&A
Approachable	Sharing questions from specific citizen groups

TONE OF VOICE	HOW TO DISPLAY IT ONLINE
Credible/ trustworthy	Reminding our citizens that we are the go-to trusted expert on this topic/in this area
Relatable	Giving over our channels to our citizens so that they speak to, and on behalf of, that larger demographic by sharing user-generated content
Knowledgeable	Protecting the truth always and ensuring citizens choose us first as the go-to expert and trusted voice
Non-preachy	Sharing knowledge and advice in a non-judgemental way
Practical	'*How-to*' content, e.g., tutorial videos
Customer-first mindset	When writing copy or creating campaigns, always thinking of our audience and not simply the corporate goals
Culture and lifestyle first	Being cognisant of the culture and lifestyle of our audiences as well as colloquial language
Affordable/ achievable	Encouraging small wins and challenges to change behaviour and to get engagement and interaction online, e.g., '*five-day challenge*'
Best in class/ excellence	We are setting the standard and we must show leadership and produce best-in-class online content to reflect the standard of our research work offline

Public voice versus peer voice

Review the make-up of your citizen sub-groups. Very often, public sector and government agencies have two main cohorts, so you must be mindful when choosing content for specific platforms, and of the language you use.

· **X%** public interest aimed at citizens
· **X%** industry professional or peers

Here is a brief guide to writing for the public (citizen voice) and writing for your peers (professional voice):

CITIZEN VOICE (HUMAN BUT PROFESSIONAL)

WRITE LIKE THIS	NOT LIKE THIS	WHY?
When Alex decided to join our Facebook Group, very quickly he realised he was empowering other Dads just like him. Changing how he thought about fatherhood gave him more confidence and a better relationship with his family. Here's what Alex had to say...	We invite Dads to join our Facebook Group, where you will get expert advice and support. Fatherhood can be a challenging time, especially for first-time Dads. Join our Group now!	We personalise our messages and we engage in a meaningful conversation. We always step into the shoes of our audience— in this case, new Dad Alex. Give Alex a voice; he represents your target audience.

PROFESSIONAL VOICE (DISPLAYING THOUGHT LEADERSHIP)

WRITE LIKE THIS	NOT LIKE THIS	WHY?
The Dad 1st campaign is an example of leveraging our audience to create a tangible programme for parents. Very often we turn research into press releases and forget whom we are trying to support and advise.	The Dad 1st campaign is a collaborative programme involving key government bodies. We are proud partners.	You need to show how you do your work; your peers know why. You should also share insights into how you approach the challenges and not just share the wins. Peer education marketing is about teaching moments of shared value.

The individual voices of your organisation

In order to scale the expert knowledge and the campaigns developed in your organisation, you should execute a plan of personalising and showing the faces and voices of the organisation. Here are a few examples of who could speak, on what topics, and through what platforms.

VOICES MATRIX

VOICES	TOPIC/S	CHANNELS/MEDIA
CEO	Corporate news/ developments	Media, conferences, events
Subject matter experts	Politics, science, public policy, health	Media, blog, contributing copy for social, videos, podcast interviews, conferences, events
Communications professionals	Consumer campaigns and trending topics	Videos, podcast hosts, conferences, events
Social media team	Repurposed expert and campaign content	Social networks
Web manager	Repurposed expert and campaign content	Website
Partners and stakeholders	Relevant topics	Contributing to blog, videos, podcasts, social media
Influencers	Relevant topics	Video, social media, podcast, blog, consumer engagement events
Ambassadors	Relevant topics	Video, social media, podcast, blog, consumer engagement events

The social media manager

Managing your social media interactions with online communities across several platforms will require a single unifying mindset and, quite possibly, an entire social customer support team.

The challenge is finding a skilled social media community manager that fits the bill. Being a great community manager is a lot like being a superhero. You are often expected to be everywhere at once, simultaneously entertaining the masses, finding new and interesting content and putting out fires driven by unhappy citizens who bring their troubles to your public platform.

A great community manager goes out to where the people are and builds an entire online community of interested and curious individuals who want to find out more about their organisation, and what the social media community has to offer.

A social media manager or community manager should be a skilled social media enthusiast with at least two years' experience managing social networks and an associated community. They should have strong skills in online reputation management and will be informed on ongoing changes to social networks.

It is a myth that social media community managers should be juniors who are adept at using all social networks. Ask yourself: would you let a junior member of staff manage your organisation's public relations activities?

Daily community management tasks

- Engage and respond to public comments on social networks (where relevant).

- Respond to private comments on social networks.

- Prompt engagement in niche groups as part of the overall content calendar (e.g., Facebook/WhatsApp Groups).

- Moderate live social events (e.g., Twitter Chats, Facebook Live, live event reporting).

- Manage mentions and tags on all social networks.

- Build visibility and credibility by attending Twitter Chats and moderating any organisation chats.

- Strategise with the social media team on ways to scale communities and connect with new people.

- Analyse efforts to drive more traffic to organisation website/ campaign landing page.

- Create online relationships with other relevant stakeholders and influencers.

- Provide community management reports to the social media manager on a monthly basis.

- Feed relevant data into the weekly digital communications meeting where appropriate.

Ongoing community management protocols

As community manager, you are responsible for activating the organisation's abuse policy when necessary. This may be because of bot-related activity, or individuals who engage in trolling online. You will need to be familiar with the organisation's Escalating Social Media Abuse Policy. See chapter 9 for more on creating your own policy for dealing with online abuse.

Chatbots are a way to engage at a deeper level with a large community on specific topics. For example, the Facebook Messenger chatbot allows you to communicate directly with service users via Messenger and now with Messenger 2.2, via your website.

Make sure you have someone monitoring social media during peak engagement times. If your organisation doesn't have a 24/7 community management rota, you should set automated messages during off-peak times, e.g., nights or weekends.

However, a system may be developed with another team member to rotate evening shifts, e.g., 6 p.m. to 9 p.m. and weekend community management.

11 essential competencies for the perfect community manager

These are the skills you need (or are looking for) to effectively manage an online community:

1. *An expansive personality*

A social media community manager isn't just someone who Tweets in the name of the organisation. In fact, you're often using your own name, and acting as a face of the organisation.

Your job is to reach out to thousands of people in their most comfortable and casual online environments and build relationships between them and the agency. A great community manager is ready to become a listening ear with every single one of the thousands of people in their social media community and to bring on board even more community members all the time.

2. *An interest in the opinions of others*

A social media community manager asks for the opinions of your online community members. This can involve posting fun questions, creating surveys or simply sparking interesting discussions on your social networks. Once the discussion or answers to questions start rolling in, your job is not done yet. A great community manager also sticks around to give friendly and helpful responses and to fuel the fire of community interaction on the topics you have provided. This creates active, constantly engaging interest and support for the brand and makes the community feel involved, listened to and valued.

3. *A friendly attitude*

Even if you really love spending time with thousands of people online, if your attitude is sour, no one will be able to detect that joy. A fantastic community manager can make everyone they talk to or who even sees their public messages feel that warm fuzzy sensation of potential friendship. Ideally, every member of your online community will feel as though you, as community manager, are their own personal friend, there to listen to and help them at any time. The friendlier your attitude is, the more friends you can make for the organisation.

4. *Creative content generation*

In social media, the community manager is responsible for writing, finding and commissioning incredibly interesting and creative content. This can be news stories, organisational behind-the-scenes information or even artistic photos of things that relate to your department. The content you post could become the next discussion topic or simply engage the community in the current goings-on with your office. The more creative you are, the more people will want to come back and read your content.

5. An eye for trends

Another important part of any social media management job is keeping an eye on trends. On Twitter especially, nothing matters more than knowing which hashtags to use, the emotional and trending topics on the platform and what issues the majority of social media users are worked up about. On the flip side, viral videos and memes also make powerful trend content for your social media marketing campaigns and will draw a lot more attention than even well-written topical insights.

6. Empathy and tact

Not every member of your online community is always going to be happy, and you can gain massive credibility as a compassionate organisation when your community manager is sensitive to the troubles of the community. Sometimes acknowledging frustration or anger can go some way to reassuring the public that you are working on their concerns. This has to be balanced with knowing when to listen and not engage.

7. Passion for the project

No matter how good a community manager is at wrangling people through social media, one of the most powerful forces is passion. You need to deeply understand and love the organisation at hand. This way, everything you say about your work will be positive, supportive and refreshingly well-informed. In fact, the best social media community managers are involved in the work somehow in their own way and can, therefore, write some very interesting and persuasive content to share with the community.

8. Resilience in the face of trolling and abuse

Most of your community members will be friendly and supportive, but there are always a few trolls and truly mean people on the

Internet. As a representative for a public sector or government agency, social media community managers are often considered sitting ducks for people who like to target someone online and make them break down, cry or admit fault for having done nothing wrong. Whether you are dealing with abusive citizens looking to hurt someone in the organisation or your average social media troll, as a great community manager, you need to comfortably let insults and irrelevant complaints roll off your shoulders while remaining fun and pleasant for everyone else. But you should be able to rely on the counsel of a colleague or line-manager if the abuse is causing you deep upset. Similarly, the organisation should have protocols in place to ensure individual staff members are supported when in the line of fire online.

9. *The ability to automate smoothly*

Automation of messages and content sharing is a major part of today's social media management tasks because, quite frankly, keeping up with a full stack of social media platforms is a big task even for an entire inbound marketing and customer services team. A good community manager will be able to adapt to the automation software available and begin gathering collections of content to post at pre-determined times in order to keep your social media feeds lively while other work gets accomplished. The key to talented social media automation is to make it seem like it isn't automated at all. This means including a dynamic variety of content and even making pre-scheduled posts send at slightly off-times, like 3:04 p.m. instead of 3:00 p.m. exactly.

10. *An understanding of grammar and punctuation*

The one hard rule about any use of social media in the name of an organisation is that great grammar is a must. Chat-speak and slang can be used for comedic effect every now and then but, officially, the community manager needs to represent the organisation in a professional manner. This means keeping your chat-speak to joke-levels only, not overusing emoticons, and remembering to mind your p's and q's when writing posts.

11. *Tech savvy on multiple platforms*

Finally, there is a lot more than one platform for social media. Whether your organisation prioritises Facebook, Twitter, LinkedIn, Instagram, YouTube, TikTok, Snapchat or all of the above, you will need to be prepared to handle messages and conversations happening on all fronts. This is the number one reason why community managers usually end up splitting up the job and delegating effectively: to ensure that the community of every social media platform gets the attention it deserves.

* * * * *

ACHIEVING BEST-IN-CLASS SOCIAL MEDIA output starts with ensuring you have the basics. Very often we know what we need to do but don't do it. Start by performing a social media audit. Then create clear, actionable goals that align with your organisation's objectives. Think of this work as a social media spring clean. Don't forget that then you need to employ a skilled social media community manager to manage the reins of public discourse.

5

Content Marketing for Government and Public Sector Agencies

What you have, that the public need and want, is information. But still agencies are reluctant to invest in content marketing as a method of communications. At a time when governmental-led information has never been more in demand, now is your opportunity to step into the void to serve with better intention.

The question I asked in the first edition of this book still holds weight today: 'Have you brought your long-form content into the Digital Age?' It is a myth that long-form content—blogs, articles, white papers, podcasts or longer video formats, for example—is dead, replaced by scrolling endlessly through social media newsfeeds. But it is true that how we tell stories has changed forever. Press releases and phone calls are now blog posts and WhatsApp messages, and in-person appointments have transformed into Zoom, Meet and Teams video calls. In this chapter we will examine the importance of long-form content for government and public sector agencies.

Content marketing is important for you because it:

- Serves a key objective around public interesting messaging.
- Demonstrates openness and transparency.

- Helps discoverability on search engines, if optimised correctly.
- Promotes trust and accountability.
- Acts as a magnet for organic website traffic.
- Is a central cog in the campaign wheel.
- Speaks to relevant and targeted audiences.
- Can be repurposed for cross-channel social media amplification.
- Triggers online conversations and feedback.
- Provides valuable expert knowledge to the public.
- Complements other government or agency programmes.
- Strikes up public dialogue on social media.
- Serves to silence and overturn misinformation.

Public interest messaging by its very nature can be detailed and complex. In order to articulate your story in its entirety, you will have to plan out the story and its relevance to specific audiences.

If you are just starting out on your content marketing journey or want to revisit your strategy, here are three steps that will keep you focused along with delivering results:

1. Map the content to the pain point of your citizens—meaning, the problem they would like to solve.

2. Then, use the right type of content for that problem.

3. Finally, map the content to the online journey of the people who have that problem.

Content marketing examples

- Landing page
- Podcast
- Episodic video series (YouTube)
- Social video (TikTok, Facebook, Twitter, LinkedIn, Instagram)
- Blog
- Dedicated website
- Digital magazine
- E-zine

- Checklist
- Original research
- White paper/report
- Quizzes/polls
- Webinars
- Interviews/Q&As
- Livestreams
- Infographics
- How-to guide
- Presentations
- Social media posts
- FAQ
- Audiograms
- Gifs

Content mapping and planning

It is important to step into the shoes of your audiences so that everything you do resonates and inspires action or behavioural change. Every digital marketing tactic you deploy online requires some form of content to support it. Now it is time to map out the content you need to create for your key audiences.

It is essential that you are clear on your pillar content, i.e., those messages that are central to shaping public opinion and engaging niche audiences in relevant conversations. Mapping out a content hierarchy will ensure you remain focused on the content that matters most to your organisation.

Your work begins at the top of the content marketing funnel, with awareness-building using search marketing, organic social media, Google pay per click (PPC) and social advertising. The content created for the top part of the funnel is aimed at getting your audience to click through into longer-form content on a website landing page. At this point, people will stay and engage, or jump off quickly if the content does not resonate with them.

CONTENT MARKETING FUNNEL

Funnel Stage	Channel	Metric
Top of Funnel (TOFU)	Social Media & PPC	REACH
Top of Funnel (TOFU)	SEO	CLICK-THROUGHS
Middle of Funnel (MOFU)	Landing Page Optimisation	TIME ON SITE
Middle of Funnel (MOFU)	Content Marketing	READERS
Middle of Funnel (MOFU)	Website Optimisation	LEADS
Bottom of Funnel (BOFU)	Email Marketing	PROSPECTS
Bottom of Funnel (BOFU)	On-Page Goals	CONVERSION
Bottom of Funnel (BOFU)	Customer Experience	LOYALTY
Bottom of Funnel (BOFU)	Testimonials	CITIZEN ADVOCATES

Review user signals

User signals provide evidence that people are interested in your content. Look at click-through rate, time on site, bounce rate and goal conversions to establish content marketing success.

- Website sessions are recorded in Google Analytics, which can tell you how long visitors engaged with the content.

- By setting up conversions on your landing page (e.g., sign-up, download, watch, register), you can record event goals that denote an action. These people are now prospects and have demonstrated to you that they want to engage further with you and your content.

- Returning visitors to your site are a sign of true audience loyalty. They become advocates when they share your content on their own social media channels.

12 key aspects of a content marketing plan

By adhering to the following 12-part blueprint, you are using the content marketing best practices of audience segmentation, content research, planning, creating, publishing and promoting.

1. *Setting content KPIS*

Be very clear on why you are creating your content, and what your key performance indicators will be from a content marketing campaign.

2. *Campaign/topic*

Establish what the campaign is about and what big topic you are addressing. As your campaign will likely be in the public interest, its success will likely be a very important piece of your organisation's objectives.

3. *Audience segmentation*

With a clear vision of the topic you are addressing, now you need to be just as clear on the audience you are targeting.

4. *Keyword research*

It is important to undertake keyword research on both YouTube and Google, ensuring that you are leveraging the available organic traffic from both search engines (the world's biggest). Include long-tail keywords in your research (see textbox on page 102).

5. *Messaging defined*

Define up to five messages for your target audience that are matched to that audience's persona profile. This will keep you focused and targeted throughout.

6. *Long-form content*

Opinions vary on what qualifies content as long-form, but here are some approximations:

- **Blog post:** 1,500+ words. Did you know the average word-count on a piece of content that ranks on the first page of Google's search engine results pages (SERPs) is 2,000 words?
- **Video:** 8+ minutes for YouTube in particular.
- **Livestream or podcast:** 10+ minutes to give depth to a topic.
- **Speech:** 10+ minutes. Did you know we speak at three words per second? So, a 10-minute speech will provide 1,800 words.

Long-Tail Keywords

HubSpot defines a long-tail keyword as 'a keyword phrase that contains at least three words (though some say two or more is considered long-tail). Long-tail keywords are used to target niche demographics rather than mass audiences. In other words, they're more specific and often less competitive than generic keyword terms.'

There are two steps to creating a list of relevant long-tail keywords:

Step 1: Brainstorm a list of relevant topics related to this campaign or issue.
Step 2: Create a list of long-tail keywords associated with that topic.

Here are two free tools you can use:

Google Predictive Search: Click on Google.com to view the related search terms that appear when you type in a keyword. When you type in your phrase and scroll to the bottom of Google's results, you'll notice some suggestions for searches related to your original input. These keywords can lead you to thinking about other relevant keywords you hadn't already considered.

Google Trends: You don't need a Google account in order to access Google Trends. Google Trends is a free service that:

- Shows you trends for your keywords.
- Helps you find content ideas.
- Shows you seasonal spikes and local differences for your keyword at a glance.
- Allows you to compare the popularity of topics and keywords.

Examples of long-tail keywords

Topic: PR Crisis Management on Social Media
Long-tail keywords for this topic:

- How to Handle a PR Crisis
- Digital PR Crisis Communications Plan

- Digital PR Crisis Management
- Online Crisis Management
- Digital PR Crisis Definition
- Digital PR Crisis Examples
- Digital PR Crisis Management Case Studies
- Company Crisis on Social Media
- Digital PR Crisis Planning
- Digital PR Crisis Plan Template
- Digital PR Crisis on Social Media

7. Lead magnet/call to action

What provides value to your audience? What would they sign up for, or share on their social networks? Offer something that your audience can't resist, such as a guide, checklist, e-book, webinar or tutorial video. Make sure your call to action is very clear and impossible to pass up.

8. The content journey

Now it is time to map out the content marketing journey, as we did with the content marketing funnel. Start by documenting the pain points or emotional triggers of your target audience. Then use the same process as you did with the funnel to map how they will find your content online.

9. Digital content calendar

Your digital content calendar will support the execution of your plan (see page 104). You should have a monthly schedule that you stick to.

10. Repurposing long-form content

When we take time to produce relevant content for a specific audience in long-form (e.g., blog article, video, podcast), we must repurpose it for greater reach and amplification across the social web. On page 106, I include some essential tips for repurposing content.

SAMPLE CONTENT REPURPOSING PLAN*

	MONDAY	TUESDAY	WEDNESDAY
WEEK 1: PODCAST	Facebook Page post Facebook Group post (motivation) Twitter posts (2) Learning hub engagement	Email marketing Facebook Page post Facebook Group post (tip) Twitter posts (2) Learning hub engagement	Facebook Page post Facebook Group post (word of the week) Twitter posts (2) Learning hub engagement
WEEK 2: LEAD MAGNET	Facebook Page post Facebook Group post (motivation) Twitter posts (2) Learning hub engagement	Email marketing (11:30 a.m.) Facebook Page post Facebook Group post (tip) Twitter posts (2) Learning hub engagement	Facebook Page post Facebook Group post (word of the week) Twitter posts (2) Learning hub engagement
WEEK 3: BLOG	Facebook Page post Facebook Group post (motivation) Twitter posts (2) Learning hub engagement	Email marketing (11:30 a.m.) Facebook Page post Facebook Group post (tip) Twitter posts (2) Learning hub engagement	Facebook Page post Facebook Group post (word of the week) Twitter posts (2) Learning hub engagement
WEEK 4: VIDEO	Facebook Page post Facebook Group post (motivation) Twitter posts (2) Learning hub engagement	Email marketing (11:30 a.m.) Facebook Page post Facebook Group post (tip) Twitter posts (2) Learning hub engagement	Facebook Page post Facebook Group post (word of the week) Twitter posts (2) Learning hub engagement

This is my own repurposing plan for my Public Sector Marketing Institute community.

THURSDAY	FRIDAY	SATURDAY	SUNDAY
Facebook Page post	Facebook Page post	Facebook Page post	Facebook Page post
Facebook Group post (tool of the week)	Facebook Group post (shout-out)	Facebook Group post (general)	Facebook Group post (general)
Twitter posts (2)	Twitter posts (2)	Twitter posts (2)	Twitter posts (2)
Learning hub engagement	Learning hub engagement	Learning hub engagement	Learning hub engagement
Facebook Page post	Facebook Page post	Facebook Page post	Facebook Page post
Facebook Group post (tool of the week)	Facebook Group post (shout-out)	Facebook Group post (general)	Facebook Group post (general)
Twitter posts (2)	Twitter posts (2)	Twitter posts (2)	Twitter posts (2)
Learning hub engagement	Learning hub engagement	Learning hub engagement	Learning hub engagement
Facebook Page post	Facebook Page post	Facebook Page post	Facebook Page post
Facebook Group post (tool of the week)	Facebook Group post (shout-out)	Facebook Group post (general)	Facebook Group post (general)
Twitter posts (2)	Twitter posts (2)	Twitter posts (2)	Twitter posts (2)
Learning hub engagement	Learning hub engagement	Learning hub engagement	Learning hub engagement
Facebook Page post	Facebook Page post	Facebook Page post	Facebook Page post
Facebook Group post (tool of the week)	Facebook Group post (shout-out)	Facebook Group post (general)	Facebook Group post (general)
Twitter posts (2)	Twitter posts (2)	Twitter posts (2)	Twitter posts (2)
Learning hub engagement	Learning hub engagement	Learning hub engagement	Learning hub engagement

11. *Publishing cross-platform*

Now it is time to publish your repurposed content on each digital channel: website, YouTube, podcast platforms, social media, email.

12. *Engaging with your digital audience*

Now that you have published your content and it is getting traction online, you must step forward to have conversations with your audiences. Don't let all your hard work up to now go to waste. Engage.

> 'Multi-channel marketing provides the content our audiences are searching for; in all the places they search.'
>
> MICHAEL BRENNER, CMO influencer

A guide to content repurposing

Repurposing is presenting content in a different way that maintains its core message, while reaching an expanded audience. Repurposing content has the following advantages:

It builds your online audiences. By constantly creating content, you are building your online audiences as they engage and convert.

It gives you authority. By creating multiple pieces of content around the same topic, you are positioning yourself as the expert voice.

It optimises SEO. You are creating more opportunities to rank in Google for important keywords. Plus, if you take your repurposed content outside your site, you can receive quality links back to your site with the added bonus of controlling the anchor text in the link. Think about how much traffic social media drives to your website.

You can reach new audiences. More often than not, our original piece of content may reach only one audience. Repurposing the content for different channels allows you to engage with another audience where they are hanging out.

It generates leads. Content is a magnet for traffic, so by repurposing it across multiple channels for greater amplification, you have more ways to attract people back to your lead magnet or landing page where you have a series of goals set up.

It reinforces your message. Repetition is an essential tactic for public interest messaging. The traditional 'marketing rule of seven' states that audiences need to hear your message seven times before they take the action you want them to. This has increased to 7–12 digital touchpoints in the Digital Age. So, repurposing goes a long way towards reaching this quota.

Say it once, share it often

By taking one topic and one long-form piece of content and repurposing it, you have multiple bite-sized pieces of content to share across all your digital channels. But you must respect the formats, tone of voice and audiences on each digital channel and customise accordingly.

1. Identify your long-form content

Your long-form content may be a blog post, report, video, speech, livestream or podcast (see page 101 for approximate lengths for each).

- **Make it evergreen:** Repurposed content should not be time sensitive. It should always be valuable to a large audience, be a core part of your work/messaging and attract interest.

- **Focus your keyword:** Make sure you have selected your long-tail keyword and a topic your audience cares about. You might look at your own website search analytics to see what content your audience engages with most.

- **Keep to your core message:** Be very clear on the core message that is going to feature in every single piece of repurposed content you produce.

2. *Repurpose it into another long-form piece of content*

By taking a blog post and creating a video, and then a podcast episode or an audio file, you are providing multiple ways for your audience to consume long-form content. Here are some examples of how single pieces of content can be repurposed for multiple long-form content channels.

Video transcribed into a blog post.

Audio from video used for a podcast episode or an embeddable SoundCloud file in your blog post.

Speech/stage presentation audio transcribed into a blog post.

Blog post turned into a YouTube video explaining the main points.

LIVE   Livestream transcribed and turned into a blog post.

3. *Use graphics that support your content*

Incorporate graphics into your blog posts, social media and email marketing. Remember to optimise all images according to each social network's guidelines. Sprout Social maintains an updated list of the graphic dimension requirements for each social network on their blog.

Here are a few examples of social and promotional graphics:

- Quote graphics
- Infographics
- Instructional images and how-to illustrations
- Blog featured image
- Stats graphic
- E-zine header graphic

Other repurposing ideas for long-form content

Video

- Repurpose snippets and stills from long-form video for social media including TikTok.

Instagram

- Take still shots from your videos and turn them into posts for Instagram. Use the summary in your captions to get more reach and send people back to your video.
- Take your audience behind the scenes with an Instagram Story promoting your long-form video.

Twitter

- Tweet your still shots, video and blog posts so you can populate your Twitter timeline with the same content. Twitter will also embed your video and your SoundCloud posts in the Tweets.

Social video

- Snip a 40-second promotional clip for Twitter, Facebook, LinkedIn and Instagram.

SlideShare

- Turn your transcript into a PDF and upload it to SlideShare so you can get backlinks to your YouTube video and blog post.

* * * * *

AS A PUBLIC SECTOR or government body, you are sitting on expertise, knowledge and valuable insights that you need to unleash to the public through your suite of digital channels.

While social media generates awareness and even engagement initially, you need the public to be fully versed in your campaign messages, and this requires producing longer-form content in different formats. Content creation can be overwhelming, but it needn't be. My approach: Say it once, share it often across your channels.

6

Digital Storytelling Techniques for Government and Public Sector Agencies

Engaging your citizens online

We are wired to remember stories. In fact, Stanford School of Business marketing professor Jennifer Aaker says that stories are up to 22 times more memorable than facts and figures alone. Stories are commanding record consumption rates. Audiences are drawn to the story behind the story: 87% would choose to watch shows online instead of on television if it meant they could see more behind-the-scenes content.

I describe myself as a storyteller. Twenty-one years ago I began my career as a broadcast journalist, sharing news stories to over 60,000 people live on radio every day. I love the power of a story. As public sector marketing pros, it is your responsibility to captivate the imagination and interest of the citizens you serve.

The explosion of storytelling across the social web has given us a feast for the visual senses. But for marketers, it is proving quite a challenge to keep up with the skills and the technology.

Digital storytelling for government and public sector means simply leveraging technology and/or online platforms to communicate to and engage citizens. This can be done through video, graphics, photos or even blogging and on social networks, wikis, blogs, websites or forums. The power of digital storytelling is that—unlike with a press release—you have the opportunity to personalise and humanise the story in a way that resonates with the reader, listener or viewer.

Because public sector and government agencies often hide behind the logo of their organisation, they are not inclined to be over-enthusiastic about storytelling. 'It's OK for you,' I remember one public sector marketing pro saying to me during one of my digital storytelling masterclasses. 'You run your own business so you can be personal, personable and bring people behind the scenes. It's all promoting you and your work.' Public sector marketing pros or official spokespeople often feel fearful of putting themselves front of screen on behalf of the organisation. As a staff member, they feel conflicted about their personal versus professional self online, and this can make them hesitant to be a face on the social web.

But there is no doubt that storytelling with engaging content is a precursor for a successful social media or digital marketing campaign. So, in this chapter, I will take you through a series of digital storytelling techniques that you can implement right away.

The Types of Digital Storytelling

Quote graphics: This involves overlaying text that quotes an individual on a photo or graphic. These are very popular on Instagram.

Photos: A picture still tells a thousand words, and research has found that using original photography (as opposed to stock or graphic designed images) is more engaging on social media.

Animation: Movement triggers a response online. Animation can take multiple formats, from gifs to cartoon-based videos to whiteboard doodles.

Short-form video: Video that is less than two minutes long is considered short-form video. Engaging citizens on particular topics on social media is enhanced with short-form video that can be a piece spoken to the camera, a vlog-style behind-the-scenes with conversation, a highlights overview, news-style reportage or an info-commercial.

Long-form video: In the previous chapter, you saw that long-form video has an important place on social media, particularly on YouTube. Vertical video on Instagram can also be up to one hour long. Embedding long-form video into your website landing page or blog post will shore up lots of relevant traffic for you.

Stories: Born on Snapchat, exploding on Instagram and TikTok and a rising star on Facebook, Stories are ephemeral—or disappearing—content that hangs around for 24 hours. You can save your Stories for reuse on another platform, e.g., sharing an Instagram Story on Facebook Stories (see page 106 for more on repurposing content).

Livestreams: Going live commands the attention of your citizens in real time. Breaking news is the number one type of live content consumed on the Internet, at 56%, and content from conferences, events and festivals stands at 43%. You can livestream on the main social networks: Facebook, Instagram, Twitter and YouTube. At the time of writing, if your account meets certain requirements, you can also go live on TikTok and LinkedIn.

Social media: Conversations are happening at an extraordinary rate on social media. It truly has become the water-cooler corner for all types of hot topics. Consider that at any given second, there are more than 9,900 Tweets sent. The key to digital storytelling on social media is to ensure you are actually engaging and not just broadcasting. (Leave your press and media team to do that job for you.) Your role is to be fully engaged in a two-way conversation.

Blogging: A blog is conversational content that appeals to the public. 'Did you know?', 'how-to' and 'why' content works well for a blog. A common mistake in public sector communications is using your website to publish press releases and corporate statements, expecting citizens to engage with it. Press releases are for journalists. (This is not to say your media statements should not be published on your website; they absolutely should.)

Podcasting: The growth of podcasting cannot be ignored. While it still reaches small audiences in some markets, audio as a medium is having a resurgence. The Edison Research Infinite Dial study reported a steady growth in podcasts and a rapid growth for smart speakers for 2019.

Webinars: Sharing knowledge or information in a video tutorial or presentation style is a powerful way to get meaningful engagement. With people having to sign up and share their email address and commit to spending an hour with you, there is no doubt it is a sure-fire way to build relationships and empower citizens with valuable knowledge and information. A webinar presents a low-cost, high-impact approach to digital storytelling.

Virtual reality: Virtual reality (VR), or computer-simulated life, creates artificial digital environments in which users can immerse themselves. VR can be used for educational or entertainment purposes. The number of active VR users hit 170 million+ in 2018.

Augmented reality: Augmented reality (AR) is similar to VR, but simply adds virtual additions on top of the real environment. Apple CEO Tim Cook has said that AR will one day be as important in our everyday lives as 'eating three meals a day.' AR is powerful because it can capture people's attention for over 85 seconds, increase interaction rates by 20% and improve click-through rates (CTR) to conversion by 33%.

Gamification: Combining traditional gaming with marketing can create an opportunity for public sector organisations to engage with the public. Using point scoring, competition with others, rules of play and challenges in an online environment is a real trigger for engagement and conversation.

Sources: Livestream.com, Internet Live Stats, Edison Research, Architosh, Business Insider, The Drum

How government and public sector agencies can incorporate storytelling

There are four tactics that public sector marketing pros can bring into their storytelling that will improve their digital outcomes. Let's call them 'the four Ps':

1. Personal

A major shift in public sector communications is that now *you* need to be the storyteller, not the organisation or the logo, the brand or the digital agency. Digital storytelling is all about engaging people, because people engage with people. There should be multiple voices, faces and authors identified within your department or organisation who will front communications online. This is not simply about providing a quotation for a press release or a soundbite for the arrival of a news team from the national broadcaster. You need a series of people willing to share their expertise in creative ways online to remain relevant in the S3 Age.

2. People

Telling compelling stories about the people you serve should be central to your communications. Every policy, campaign, decision or piece of legislation will affect people, and the guaranteed way to engage them in this is to put them at the centre of your story.

3. Priority

Government and public policy always have a priority issue. Creating stories around your priorities will not only command attention, but also involve the public in a way that helps them understand your position.

4. Passion

Passion is not for the few. Agreed, public policy, policing or politics can't compete with A- or Z-list celebrity news, cats or unicorns on the social web. But you must be passionate about what you share in the form of a story. Injecting passion and conviction into your words will ensure more people take an interest and share your story online.

15 digital storytelling techniques

It can be difficult to constantly come up with ideas for digital story-telling, but here are 15 guaranteed ways you can increase traffic and engagement:

1. Opinion

This content type does exactly what it suggests—it is an opinion piece about a topical issue that is in the news, on the agenda in government or dominating social media conversations.

Primary platform: YouTube.
Secondary platform: 40-second impact statement soundbite on Twitter.

2. How-to guides

This type of content shows your community how to do something by sharing step-by-step tips and screenshots, videos and images.

Primary platform: In written format, share as a PDF e-book and/or as a video on YouTube, both embedded onto your website.

Secondary platforms: Export the top knowledge bombs and share as statistical or quote graphics on social media. A behind-the-scenes with an expert on Stories would also work (depending on the target audience, of course).

3. Comparison

In this content, you compare political ideologies on a particular topic, public services in another country/countries, theses or experiences.

Primary platform: Blog post.
Secondary platform: YouTube piece to camera.

4. Lists

This content shares a list of reasons, ways or tips on how to do something. These are very popular as they can be provided in easy-to-read, bite-sized chunks of information.

Primary platform: Blog post.
Secondary platforms: List entries repurposed for social media.

Did You Know?

MOZ AND BUZZSUMO teamed up to find out which content is most valuable in terms of social shares and backlinks. They found that list posts and videos on average achieve a higher number of social shares than other formats. According to their study, you are more likely to gain likes and shares with longer articles (over 1,000 words) and with the following formats:

· List posts
· Why posts
· How-to posts
· Videos

Source: moz.com

5. Expert view roundups

This type of content shares the views of a number of experts on one relevant or timely topic.

Primary platform: Blog post.
Secondary platform: Podcast.

6. News-jacking

In this content type, you simply write about what everyone is talking about. Write about a current news or political event that is relevant to your work. What is big in the news right now, and what can you add to it?

Primary platform: Twitter (making sure to include the news-making hashtags).
Secondary platform: Blog (for more in-depth or at-length analysis).

7. Resources

Probably everything we need or want to know about any topic is available on the Internet. However, we are all time-strapped, so it is really helpful when somebody makes the effort to compile a resource-led post; for example, the top podcasts for new mums looking for breastfeeding support and inspiration.

Primary platform: Blog post.
Secondary platform: Podcast.

8. Profiles

We all love to get to know the people behind a campaign or policy. So, doing an in-depth profile of a key individual in your organisation can help engage citizens on a particular topic.

Primary platform: Stories (choose the platform to match the target audience).
Secondary platform: Video blog.

9. Reviews

Is there a new programme, initiative or piece of legislation that you can review? Why not tell your online community what you think about it while explaining in it in lay terms? They will most likely take your advice.

Primary platform: Facebook Live.
Secondary platforms: Podcast or blog.

10. Checklists

Everybody loves a checklist! A checklist shows your knowledge and expertise in a particular subject matter.

Primary platform: Blog.
Secondary platform: YouTube.

11. Interviews

Why not use your blog as a place to interview other politicians, policy makers or experts in a particular subject? So rather than sharing your opinion and knowledge all the time, give your blog over to an interviewee who you think will be interesting to your audience.

Primary platform: Podcast.
Secondary platform: YouTube.

12. Infographics

Infographics are graphical depictions of statistical or fact-based information, and they are very easy to read and consume.

Primary platform: Pinterest.
Secondary platform: Embed on your website.

13. Videos

In 2021, 82% of the content on the Internet was video. With this in mind, we must all be prepared to make and use video content. Use video frequently in your blog posts, as it is now the most pervasive content type on the social web.

Primary platform: YouTube for SEO and discoverability and embedding into your website.
Secondary platforms: Repurposed into short-form video for social networks (relevant to your target audience).

14. Podcasts

Podcasting is a highly engaging and accessible form of content. The proliferation of smartphones and Internet access means that people are consuming personalised content on the go and at a time of their choosing. Facebook rolled out Facebook Live Audio in mid-2021 across its platform.

Primary platform: SoundCloud.
Secondary platforms: Syndicated to all podcast platforms, such as Google Play, Google Podcasts, Spotify, iHeartRadio and iTunes using Libsyn.

15. Guest posts

Why not invite other experts to write content for your blog? Most bloggers will be delighted to have the invitation.

Primary platform: Blog.
Secondary platform: Facebook Live.

* * * * *

WE DON'T REALLY HAVE the choice to not fully immerse ourselves in digital storytelling. The real questions are about the options available to us, and how well we do it.

It is time to look at your content and the conversations you want to have, and then decide how best to create the content for that platform. The ways of engaging and inspiring citizens through communication and conversation remain the same. But we have to re-think how we create and publish our content for the smartphone generation. Stories, livestreams and Twitter Chats are all new forms of communications that we didn't have even a decade ago.

How to Integrate Social and Live Video Into Government and Public Sector Communications

Tactics to go front of screen to engage the public and transform opinion

Social video is one of the most effective ways to connect with your audience. Video is shifting social media behaviour and dominating platform and algorithm changes.

Videos are great because they catch the eye, inspire curiosity and are easy to watch with a few minutes of free time. We live in remarkable times, where we can upload our videos onto multiple social media platforms rather than simply hosting them on YouTube. Story trends are also taking centre stage, and the more entertaining topic-related videos you can produce, the more interest you can stir up in your audience.

Achieving meaningful engagement is a constant challenge for public sector marketing pros, but you have no choice but to embrace video—social, live and evergreen—in your social marketing strategies. In this chapter, I will go over the best ways to create videos, what equipment to use and how to share them. Because if you don't tell your own story and share it with your dedicated social followers, you might start losing them.

Social video and marketing

Social video is an increasingly critical component of any digital marketing strategy for government and public sector. With the majority of online traffic coming from video in the near future, this content form must become part of your marketing mix to really engage citizens. Because you are in the business of public interest messaging and improving public service provision, the video marketing statistics that follow are almost like a business case for your senior leadership to invest in social video training, equipment and technology.

1. Social video appeals to the TikTok generation

We are living in a mobile-first world. This fact should be the start, middle and end when you are creating social video. TikTok's growth and influence means that you need to be including it in your social media strategy and leveraging the education and life hack content themes. In 2022, it's estimated that 82% of all global Internet traffic will come from video views and downloads. This is a 10% increase in traffic from the 72.3% accounted for in 2017.

2. Social video is immersive and engaging

Social media users are watching 100 minutes of video per day. This is a 49% increase from the 67 minutes estimated five years ago in 2018. Video content is the driving factor behind increased levels of social media engagement and website traffic. Public sector marketing pros need to make video a core part of their digital storytelling strategy because of its ability to convince and convert. Moreover, consumers want more video, and advertisers are investing in both the production of video and in advertising campaigns to promote that video content.

3. Social networks are prioritising video views

Most of the social networks' algorithms are now giving priority to video content as well as constantly adding new video capabilities. This trend will continue, and as marketers we need to understand how social video is improving engagement, along with the impact it is having on conversions.

Did You Know?

ACCORDING TO THE cloud-based video creation service Animoto:

- '92% of marketers use assets and content they already have to make videos.'

- 'Marketers feel the most confident about reaching customers with video on Facebook and YouTube. Consumers are still viewing on these platforms, but are also starting to expand the platforms where they're watching branded video content. The top three channels they're watching videos from brands are Facebook, Instagram Stories, and Snapchat.'

Source: Animoto

The ABCs of social video storytelling

So, how do you create a video to share on social media, anyway? It all starts with a story. The public are more engaged than ever on topics that interest them. As a public sector marketing pro, you will be very well aware of what their triggers are in the context of your work.

Whether it is public health, transport disruption, political debate or crime and disorder, you have the attention of the public.

Why not maximise this attention with video, shaping public opinion with your own story? Video that also personalises a topical or controversial issue will demonstrate transparency and a willingness to keep people informed.

Here are a few steps to get started on producing video content:

Step 1: Have a strong starting point

It is not the story that matters; it is how you tell it... so the saying goes. Well, maybe the story does matter—but no matter how awesome your story is, if you don't tell it well, nobody will pay attention. In order to turn that wonderful idea into a video that people will actually care about and want to watch, you must start with a strong foundation. That means writing down what the content of your video should include. It means making a plan that you can follow, and sticking to that plan.

Some great starting points include:

- A good script.
- Several great interview questions, and an expert lined up to interview.
- Clearly outlined key points.
- A developed message.

Clarify what will be in your video and what you hope to accomplish with the video. Then, it's time to fill in the details.

Step 2: Build the details into the story

This is what separates an amateur videographer from a professional producer. You're almost ready to start shooting, but first, take a deeper look at these details of your story:

- **Characters:** Relatable characters are key to gathering interest. If your viewers can't relate with the characters, they won't watch the video. Even the most bizarre personalities of YouTube are relatable to viewers, because they share their sense of humour and speak their generational language.

- **Tone:** A fully developed tone sets the mood of the video, and helps you connect with your viewers on an emotional level. Is the tone of your video consistent with your brand voice? Is it consistent with itself?

- **Setting:** Choose a setting that works with the tone of your video, looks professional and resonates with your viewers.

- **Lighting:** Although it is easily overlooked if you have never done a video before, lighting is a critical element to the professionalism of your video. Use plenty of overhead lights if you are shooting indoors, or wait until you have a clear, sunny day to film outside. A lot of your message gets lost if your viewers have trouble seeing you or your content.

- **Clean up:** The finishing tasks of producing a video are often best left to people who know exactly what they are doing if you want a high-end finish. If you want to scale video internally, why not invest in easy-to-edit software that anyone can become proficient in.

Step 3: Storyboard your video

Creating a storyboard before you start producing your video will help ensure your content is truly telling a start-to-finish story. Here are the elements you should include:

- **Opener:** The opener needs to grab your viewer's attention immediately. It needs to intrigue them and encourage them to keep watching. Aim to establish a sense of urgency or mystery in your opener to retain their interest.

- **Problem to solve:** The problem statement promotes the issue facing the viewer. Be mindful as to who your target audience is so that you tailor your message.

- **Solution:** You have hooked the viewer with an intriguing opener. They are curious for more knowledge or information. Then you connected with them by recognising their problem. Now is the time to show the viewer how you can solve their specific problem. Here's where you'll go into more detail.

- **Call to action (CTA):** Finally, the CTA is where you literally ask the viewer to take a specific action—filling out a lead form, visiting their website, registering your interest.

If your video is not already compelling enough, you can then add in a testimonial. Make sure your brand name, website address and CTA are all clear on the final frame of your video and linger long enough for the viewer to process.

The three types of video

Depending on how timely your message is or how immediate you want to be, there are three ways you can create video content:

1. Social video

Pre-recorded video for any of the social networks that is optimised and captioned will serve your audience and your organisation well. Pre-recorded video can be batch-produced and put on scheduled release.

2. Live video

Choosing a livestream as your video tactic must have a good enough reason to justify it. Being present in the moment to a viewing audience requires planning and preparation.

3. Evergreen video

Evergreen video is worth its digital weight in gold as you produce video content that is relevant today, tomorrow and even in 12 months. To prepare a video plan of evergreen content, I suggest you do an A–Z library of essential information that the public need from you. This content probably already exists within your organisation or department, and you will just need to repackage it into video content that sits on your YouTube channel.

Video Storytelling Requires Skill

A good video marketing campaign requires excellence and time. It also takes skills and proper equipment. Investing in in-house mobile-video training will be an asset that will take your organisation to the next level of digital storytelling for citizen engagement.

Essential equipment for video storytelling

Here is a list of essential mobile-video equipment to help you get better results while filming:

1. Tripod

There is nothing more distracting to an audience than shaky footage during an interview. No matter how good you are with a camera, there is no way you will be able to shoot an interview handheld without your smartphone shaking. The best way to avoid this shaking is to purchase a tripod. It doesn't have to be a large tripod—even a light travel tripod will do, as you are only using it to hold your phone—but it will make a difference to the finished quality of your footage.

You will also need to purchase a selfie-stick phone holder. You can remove the phone holder from it and use this to attach your phone to your tripod.

2. External mic

I would advise purchasing an external mic for your smartphone. There isn't a smartphone on the market that has good enough audio recording to be able to really use it for broadcast. The RØDE VideoMic Me is made especially for smartphones and gives great sound quality.

3. External hard drive

This is not an essential part of the video process, but if you are doing a lot of filming you will find that your computer's hard drive can fill up pretty quickly. With hard drives not that expensive, it might be worth picking up a back-up.

4. 64G mini SD card (Samsung only)

If you are using a Samsung device for filming, consider buying a 64G mini SD and using this as your media drive for filming. Apart from the fact it means your phone's resources are not being used to store the video, you can also use the SD card for direct file download by putting it into your computer's card reader, which will transfer files quicker than using the USB charger lead. This means that you won't max out your smartphone's memory after just a week of filming. USBs are also becoming redundant on some devices.

Social video platforms

There are many platforms that let you make videos for your website or social media sites. The trick to getting the most out of video marketing is knowing which platforms to use for your audiences. YouTube, Facebook, TikTok, Twitter and Instagram each have their own features, functionality, benefits and quirks.

When creating video for social media, it is a great idea to repurpose your video for cross-platform promotion. For example, I always use my long-form YouTube video as the main piece of content, from which I then take snippets for the other social networks.

Think about where your audience is, and edit your video to suit the specific market:

Twitter: media, industry-specific commentators

Facebook: general public (targeted messages to specific demographics)

Instagram: younger audiences/female

LinkedIn: academic, business, sector-specific professional leadership

YouTube: curious and informed

Website: where your social media audiences arrive for more information

Best practices for leading social video platforms

YouTube

We'll start with YouTube, as this is the oldest and largest video-sharing site, with over two billion unique monthly visitors. Even if YouTube has billions of users, you don't have to be a one-in-a-billion kind of person to reap the benefits of marketing on YouTube. You do, however, have to be good at storytelling and creating consistent content.

Here is how you can build a foundation of success:

1. *Think about your viewership*

Successful online marketing, regardless of the medium, relies on providing valuable content for your target audience. Before you invest one cent in video and editing equipment, identify who will be watching your videos and who you want to watch your videos. What type of content will you produce? And how will your YouTube channel distinguish itself from the competition?

2. *Volume counts*

Many factors lead to YouTube success (or failure), but one YouTube marketing tactic is more important than all the rest: volume. It is also the simplest strategy to put in action, yet so many YouTube entrepreneurs, vloggers and marketers don't do it because it requires consistency and patience. Producing weekly content on YouTube is a minimum requirement to build an engaged audience. If you publish daily, you are going to significantly increase your chances of success.

3. *Consistency trumps creativity*

Before moving forward with a YouTube marketing campaign, evaluate your commitment to the project by considering the following:

- Are you willing to commit the necessary time to creating videos consistently?

- Will you continue to create videos when initial results might not validate the time spent?

- Do you have enough content to post consistently?

- Are you willing to take the time to promote your video correctly, depending on the platform?

Answering 'yes' to the above questions means you are ready to start.

Here are a few more YouTube tips to keep in mind:

- Your caption is important. Use a catchy title for your video, consider keywords and include a thorough description of the content.

- Add clickable links to your YouTube videos. These 'annotations' help viewers navigate this video platform to find more videos, playlists or channels.

- Use royalty-free sound effects. YouTube has its own free music library, or you can use services such as Audio Library or Free Stock Music.

- Embed YouTube videos on your website.

YouTube Live

In addition to traditional videos, livestreaming lets you engage with viewers in real time. With YouTube Live, you can broadcast live events, webinars and Hangouts from your desktop or webcam. YouTube Live is a powerful feature, especially if you already have an active YouTube channel. With 1,000 subscribers you can now go live on mobile, too.

Here are some best practices for YouTube Live:

- Create short 'trailer' videos—previewing a press conference, event or interview. Providing the big news as a takeaway is a good way to hook people in to watching for longer.

- Use relevant categories and keywords in the live events dashboard— think search engine optimisation.

- If you monetise YouTube videos, you can also do so with live events by linking to Google AdSense.

- Publicise your live video events by sharing the link on your website and social channels.

- Be aware of different time zones. Choose an optimal time to broadcast to your intended audience. You will have to test this to establish the optimal time for your videos.

- Create regular broadcasts—frequency and consistency increase subscribers and viewers.

Facebook native video

Since Facebook is the largest social media site, it makes sense that posting videos there is a good place to gain lots of exposure. While Facebook's algorithms are making it harder and harder to get posts noticed, Facebook native videos get more reach than other types of content.

Here are some tips to keep in mind when using Facebook native video:

- Upload videos directly to Facebook, rather than posting a link to a different platform, like YouTube.

- Don't forget a caption with a thorough description, a catchy title and SEO keywords.

- Facebook videos in the newsfeed will automatically start playing by default, so it is important to have a compelling opening so users don't quickly scroll past your content.

- Embed Facebook videos on your website.

- Keep videos short (60–120 seconds max) because video view retention times on Facebook are much shorter than on YouTube. Longer livestreams of five minutes or more are perfect for Instagram or Facebook.

- Add closed captions to native video because 85% of people view videos with the sound off on Facebook. Most social networks add this feature as standard now, and even on Stories text-to-speech captioning is available on Facebook, Instagram and TikTok.

DESPITE THE CONTINUED popularity of YouTube, TikTok has overtaken Facebook in the short-form video popularity stakes. What's also interesting about TikTok's growth is that users are not just watching—they are also publishing. Normally, people download multiple apps but rarely use them, but that is not the case with TikTok.

Going further than simply creating, TikTok users are collaborating. A trending feature of the app is reaction videos, where users react to a video they've seen with their own video response. Data from a Global-WebIndex study shows that over 40% of users have made a reaction video. Similarly, users are also creating Duets, which add to an original video, while 54% of users leave comments.

Source: GlobalWebIndex

Facebook Live

If you want to connect with your Facebook friends and followers in real time, the live video streaming feature is a great idea. Here's how to start:

- Promote your livestream in advance by using Facebook Stories to prime your audience. You can also use the Facebook Scheduling Tool to promote the livestream on your page. As a Page Admin, you can click on 'Publishing Tools', then click on 'Video Library' and then 'Live'. Here, you will describe your live broadcast before clicking 'Schedule'. You can add a custom image, and set the time and date that you will be live. Your fans will then be able to click the 'Reminder' call to action button to be notified of your livestream.

- Make sure your Internet connection is strong, and test before the livestream proper. This is a common error made by livestreaming beginners.

- Write a strong description to get your viewer's attention and demonstrate why they need to tune in.

- Remind your audience that they can tap on the 'Follow' button on live videos and videos that were live, then opt-in to get notifications the next time you go live.

- Be ready to go: don't have people waiting for you to check your mics, adjust your camera, etc. When the camera is on, *you are on*. Do your preparation in advance.

- Welcome viewers by name and read out their comments/questions intermittently during the broadcast.

- Interact with your audience by answering their questions. Prompt viewers to ask questions in comments and you can respond verbally. There are third-party tools for this, such as BeLive, Ecamm Live and OBS Studio.

- Remind people of the opportunity to replay, as that is how most will view it, and the reminder will give those viewers context.

- Ask people to share on their timeline and tag friends for greater reach and engagement.

- Facebook recommends that you go live for at least 10 minutes, and you can stay live for up to four hours.

Twitter Live

Twitter Live is especially effective if you're already active on Twitter and have a large following. However, you can also use it to build your following. The best way to use Twitter Live is to integrate it with your Twitter campaigns. Here are a few best practices:

- Promote your livestream in advance on Twitter.

- Give your livestream a dedicated hashtag so that people will amplify the broadcast for you.

- Get straight to the point and use a catchy video CTA.

- Turn on Twitter sharing to automatically share the broadcast.

- Respond to comments.

- Use two devices to dual stream, e.g., use a laptop and a smartphone to livestream to Twitter and Facebook at the same time.

Top Tip: A Useful Video Tool

USE ZOOM.US FOR interview-style video with remote guests. This program lets you broadcast to various platforms directly from your desktop.

Snapchat Stories

Snapchat is now most popular amongst younger teens (13–16). Snapchat Stories let you broadcast photos and short videos (up to 10 seconds) that are only available for 24 hours. Stories are good for personal branding and giving viewers an intimate look at aspects of your life or business.

Here is how you should approach the platform:

- Have a definite theme or, as the name suggests, story, as this will give you a focus and provide a clear narrative for the viewer. As it is a closed social network, keywords do not have any SEO impact.

- Overlay text on your Snaps, which you can get creative with by using the various text styles (e.g., classic, big text, label, glow or script).

- Use filters and stickers for better engagement to entice viewers to interact and spend more time viewing your Stories.

Instagram

Instagram is still experiencing exponential growth and it has massively leaned into video in the past year and continues to do so. Instagram intends video to be more native across the app and removed IGTV and added Reels. Here are some of your best options, and how to use them:

1. *Video posts*

You can post short videos to Instagram of up to 60 seconds. You can also share these videos on Twitter and Facebook.

2. *Reels*

Reels are now front and centre of the Instagram mobile app, after a 2021 re-design, and as a direct consequence of TikTok's increase in market share.

3. *Instagram Stories*

Instagram Stories, modelled on the Snapchat feature with the same name, lets you post photos and 15-second videos that disappear after

24 hours. If you post several times per day, the content gets grouped in slideshow format. This is a good feature to get attention from your followers, as Stories appear at the top of users' feeds and are more noticeable than ordinary posts. You can also highlight, or pin, certain Stories to the top of your Instagram profile.

4. Live

You can stream live on Instagram for up to one hour.

10 ways to build an engaging video series

Over time, it has been found that while one-off videos can be a hit, the best way to make the most of your cinematographic efforts is to create a series that your online audience can come back to again and again. This method sits very well with government and public sector given the vastness of your content vault, even if it's not labelled and organised. When you provide a predictable, episodic format with a constant stream of interesting content, your viewers may even start working your videos into their weekly or monthly routine; they will be able to not only enjoy your promotional material but also look forward to future episodes. This will keep your citizens engaged as they expect the next show.

The only question is what kind of series, or series collection, you should make. This can be shaped by the mandate of your organisation, your workplace culture and the tastes or needs of your audience. If you are not sure where to start, here are 10 styles of social video that have already found success among Internet communities.

1. Interview your staff

Believe it or not, your organisation's employees are one of your best sources of social media content. Digital Age citizens aren't looking for actors in make-up parroting your current catch-phrase, they want real, genuine and authentic human connection.

There are a number of creative ways to offer this kind of realistic content in your videos, and one of the best is simply to use the assets you have on hand: a series of interviews with real people who work for your organisation and are immersed in its mission.

Take a camera around your office and interview employees in each department. Ask them to explain what they do and share what they love about the work. This is not just good PR; it is also subtle advertising for your organisation as a great employer.

2. Host a talk show

Another way to bring that human touch to your social videos is to host interviews in a slightly more formal fashion. A talk show will bring front of screen your senior leaders (or identified subject matter hosts) who have an authority in a particular area, and this will build trust over time.

With a regular host or two, you can bring in all sorts of interesting names who are relevant to your sector, along with current employees, industry or government partners, key voices from the public or anyone else you think might be interesting on camera or enlightening to your citizens. The most important factor here is to make sure the interview is as real and informative as possible.

Don't be afraid to be relaxed and conversational, share a few 'industry or topic insights', and encourage your guests to be candid during the interview. This will invite your audience into your world in a recognisable setting. The host and the talk show set will serve as the episodic anchor while the guests can be your flavour content of the week.

3. Build a how-to series

Internet users spend more than 20 million hours watching how-to videos monthly. Video searches using the words 'how to' grew 70% from 2017 to 2018. So, what might your audience or potential audience need help with?

YouTube's success has been extraordinary if we consider that seemingly ordinary people are amassing massive online tribes from the comfort of their home. There is one very telling reason for this. Major brands and public sector organisations failed to create the real-life content and authentic conversations that people craved. But it is not too late for government agencies to take back their space online.

With the 'how-to' technique, you can showcase your knowledge and expertise while helping out your audience. They will tune in every week for your latest how-to social video if it meets a need.

4. Behind-the-scenes glimpses

Another great approach is the ability to take your camera absolutely anywhere that doesn't specifically display private or proprietary information. Like with the 'how-to' trend, today's audience is much more interested in what goes on behind the scenes of an organisation than in previous decades.

You might be surprised just how interested your citizens are in what goes into delivering your services, and little insights that are normally only attainable through years of hard work and experience in a certain sector. Simply by sharing these fascinating and normally exclusive tidbits of behind-the-scenes information, you can pique the curiosity of thousands into watching the next episode of your social video series.

5. Promote a campaign

Before TV remotes, digital recorders and online video consumption, organisations forced humans to sit through 2–3 minutes of promotional videos once or twice while enjoying their favourite TV shows. These were called public service announcements, and they were very annoying. For those of you who have children aged anywhere from 2 to 12, you will have heard them moan about TV ads and PSAs because they are not used to them.

If your promotional video on YouTube is done poorly, people won't hate you for interrupting their favourite show. They'll do something worse: they'll ignore you.

The Top Characteristics of a Great Promotional Video

1. **Personal bond:** These are your people. They're your audience. Bond with them.

2. **Movement:** Talking Heads is a moderately successful band from the '80s, and a horrible way to create successful promo videos. Viewers get bored just watching a talking head!

3. **Curiosity:** Make viewers curious by posing a question or presenting a problem that needs to be solved.

4. **Offer:** Entice viewers by giving them a special offer, one they get because they are taking the time to watch your video.

5. **Just like me:** Creating resonance and relevance will trump all other tactics, if your content speaks perfectly to your target audience.

6. **Value:** Just in case you forgot, the purpose of any marketing video is to provide value for your target audience.

7. **Call to action:** Somebody just spent two to four minutes watching you promote a service. They are ready to take action.

8. **Memorable tagline:** They will think about you when it is time to make a choice.

6. Collect testimonials

Testimonials have long since been an important part of any marketing suite, especially if you can get a truly happy member of the public on video. In the age of online ratings and reviews, nothing is more persuasive than a fellow citizen looking genuinely pleased on camera and speaking highly of both your service and your organisation. Think about who you can collect testimonials from, e.g., citizens who have changed their health, registered to vote or sought out new ways of tackling recycling.

While your social video campaign shouldn't be 100% testimonials, as this can start to look a little contrived, having a segment for testimonials or throwing one in for about every five videos is a great way to build the human-interest element and increase the influence of your entire series.

7. Discuss popular topics

When creating social video for a public sector organisation, first it is important to realise that you are actually marketing to people. Consider your target audience as managers or mothers rather than simply consumers. The best way to appeal to this group is by focusing on your specific know-how and cutting-edge public interest knowledge. You can do that by hosting a social video series addressing current industry news, sharing tips and focusing on popular topics you've identified on social media.

8. Humanise your department or organisation

Just as audience members are looking for that genuine human touch in how you present the content, you can also make your organisation as a whole seem more human and friendlier by focusing on interesting personal stories that happen with the staff and changes going on inside the department. Possible human-interest stories might include a staff member who gets a new puppy, or the after-work pursuits or volunteer efforts of members of the senior leadership.

Not only will your audience be moved by the personal stories of joy and goodwill, they will also have an easier time seeing your organisation as being made up of relatable, likeable people rather than a big faceless entity.

9. Share announcements

We know that you probably don't have an announcement to make every single week, but when you do, don't hesitate to make a video about it. All too often, public sector and government agencies do impressive things and hold a press conference, but the news only goes as far as people who read the news, which is a much smaller percentage of the population than it used to be.

If you want to reach your entire audience, don't forget to share with your social media circles, in the best way possible, a fun and energetic video that shows off not only what the announcement is, but why you made it and the effects it will have on the community.

10. Showcase events

Some of the best things you can possibly make a social video about are fun events hosted by your department. Whether you are launching an annual report, celebrating the appointment of a new CEO or simply showcasing the launch of a project, your audience wants to know.

By creating videos of your events, especially those where your local audience was invited, you let the rest of your supportive online community join in the fun. In fact, you might even consider live-streaming your events for exactly this purpose.

* * * * *

OF COURSE, YOU DON'T have to choose just one type of social video series. Most organisations put together a fun collection of styles unified by one- or two-episode formats so as to convey a collection of messages and reach a widespread audience.

How to maximise the results of your videos

Even if your videos are batch-produced and pre-recorded, a bit of planning before you get started will help you customise them and maximise the results of each one. In order to produce a good, engaging video, follow these steps:

1. **Find out precisely what your audience needs or wants to know.** The purpose of the video is to solve a problem.

2. **Create a detailed script.** This is particularly true for how-to or other explanations, as describing how to do something requires specific and clear instructions.

3. **Capture the viewer's attention.** There are more than five billion videos viewed on YouTube every day. If you want a viewer to stick around, give them a reason as soon as possible.

4. **Keep things simple.** Do not overwhelm viewers with overly complicated information. Stick to the basic features and offer additional videos for more detail, if necessary.

5. **Provide a call to action.** An individual just watched an entire video, a video that enlightened them or helped them solve a problem. Now what? Invite them to subscribe, visit your site, watch another video, or do something, *anything* that brings them closer to your organisation.

6. **Ask for a sub.** Don't forget to ask your viewers to like, subscribe and tap the bell for notifications when new videos are published.

And here are a few final things to consider if you want to get the best possible results from your videos:

- Plan out your video topics based on Google and YouTube keyword research.

- Be clear on the main points to be communicated in each video— for each one, stick to one topic, with three key messages.

- Decide on your video platform or social network for each video, which will inform duration and format.

- Have a studio set-up that has ample lighting, works for your audio and has a backdrop that blends as opposed to distracts.

- Show confidence and be a competent messenger on screen.

- Look down the lens, and know where the camera is—especially if using a smartphone—so that your eyeline is aligned with the viewer's.

* * * * *

THE TIME HAS PASSED to even consider if you will incorporate video into your digital communications strategy—you have to. So decide: what kind of social video is best for your organisation? Think about your citizens, your corporate voice and the message you want to convey. Which platform will you use? Mix up social, live and evergreen videos, and don't forget the power of repurposing video for greater amplification and reach.

8

How to Build Public Trust
Online: Case Studies

The transformation from 'post-and-go'
to meaningful engagement

CX is a modern phrase; it stands for 'customer experience', and of course we are talking about it in the context of online customer care for government and public sector.

I predict that call centres will eventually become digital hubs where DMs (direct messages), PMs (private messages) and instant messaging will be the CX driven by citizen demand. After all, just take a look at our own experience as consumers right now.

How are you engaging with utility companies, retail outlets, your GP and other important services? I bet in the past week you have engaged at least one service provider online and expected a same-day if not same-hour response.

These customer expectations are now spilling over into the public sector as social media and messaging communications overtake phone calls, letters and, in some sectors, emails.

So what is Social CX in public sector?

It is the ability to communicate in real time with citizens on multiple digital channels with access to the right information at the right time to answer the right questions. Easy, right? No!

Did you know that most government agencies underperform when it comes to customer satisfaction?

CUSTOMER SATISFACTION SCORES

From 1 (Very Dissatisfied) to 10 (Very Satisfied)

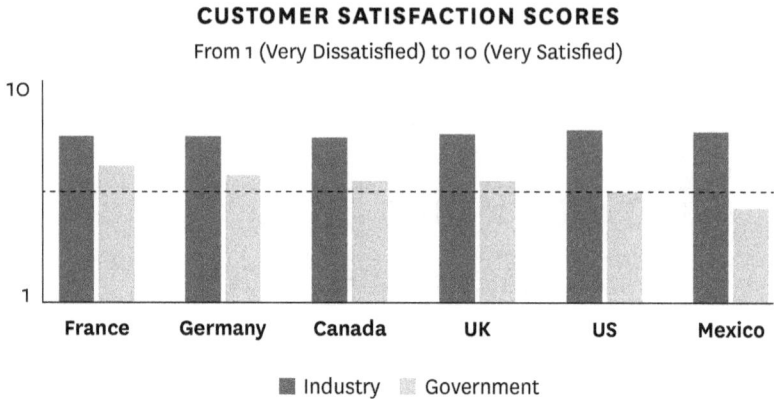

■ Industry   Government

Source: Data cited by McKinsey

A series of articles by McKinsey on this topic says that the biggest challenges facing public sector around CX are four-fold:

1. **A monopolistic mindset** is a pervasive obstacle. When customers don't have a choice, it dramatically removes a major incentive for governments to innovate and improve service. It also hampers agencies' ability to set priorities.

2. Unlike private sector organisations, government agencies must aim to serve everyone within their mandated mission; they can't just ignore certain customer segments. This bar for fairness often solidifies over time into a principle of **providing one-size-fits-all service.**

3. Governments often **lack the capabilities** needed to assess and address gaps in customer experiences. Those with **deep analytics skills, as well as human-centred design skills,** are often in short supply.

4. The **data that agencies rely upon are typically incomplete or sequestered in silos.** Thus, agencies often lack a full, timely picture of the customer's overall experience.

In reality the mindset of 'our customers don't have a choice because this is how we provide our service' won't cut it anymore.

Citizens are familiar with everyday customer service from Amazon and Apple and will make that their barometer across the customer service board.

So what are the Social CX trends that are keeping citizens happy and what should you be aiming for?

Zendesk, a company dedicated to great customer care, did a study. They reviewed data from 90,000 businesses using Zendesk across 175 countries. They compared how they use Zendesk with opinions from customers, agents, customer experience leaders and technology buyers. Using these insights, they identified this year's top trends in customer experience.

Zendesk says there are five key trends driving satisfaction in 2022:

1. **Spotlight on cx:** The rapid move towards online engagement has reshaped what customers expect from service interactions, and 75% of customers will spend more money to buy from a company that offers good CX.

2. **A more conversational world:** Customers want it all. They're flocking to social messaging and exploring new buying habits— changing their behaviour for good; 64% of customers started using a new customer service channel in 2020.

3. **Emphasis on agility:** Facing continued volatility, teams must find ways to adapt to the new needs of their customers and employees; 85% of teams reported having to make changes to their support in 2020.

4. **The Future of Work is now:** Support teams have seen a lot of change, and new pressures are forcing companies to rethink how employees work; 50% of teams reported going fully remote in 2020.

5. **The digital tipping point:** Companies are rapidly adding tools to help them scale their operations, personalise conversations, prioritise employees and meet customers where they are; 75% of decision makers say COVID-19 has accelerated their adoption of digital tech.

CASE STUDY: What Does Great
Social CX Look Like in the Digital Age?

Interview with Russel Lolacher, director of digital communications at the British Columbia Ministry of Transportation

'User experience, for those who may not know, is where we talk to users (i.e., customers, the public) about how we're doing in web properties.'

Creating a Social CX manifesto

'Right out of the gate, we created a manifesto. We had a vision and purpose statement that were very customer centric. I've had the same staff for 10 years and the culture we have created and the values we share around citizen-centred communications are certainly among some of the main reasons that people don't want to leave. They also don't get to do what we do anywhere else to the capacity that we do it.

'Things are shifting and things are moving because that's the way the world works but we needed to have a philosophy of customer first. Customer centricity is the term. For every decision we make, we need to ask, Why would they care? Who are we helping? Who are we serving? There was a UX [user experience] exercise we did eight, nine years ago.

'Defining our approach to Social CX was very important and one of the pieces of feedback that we heard in the early days from a citizen has stayed with me ever since, *"You didn't write this for me, you wrote this for yourselves."*

'I wrote that on my whiteboard and it has been there for nine years. Now anytime I'm pitched with an idea, I ask, "Who is that for?" Is it for me and you? If so, that's not our audience. So, who's it for? Anything we do we craft for the audience we're trying to serve. We're checking the metrics. We're seeing what people are responding to educational-wise. We're looking at the questions the public are asking and if they're asking a lot of the same questions, that means we have not created content or a website that answers those questions.

'The most important thing I want to do to help my ministry, my organisation, is less phone calls, less emails, because I'm doing a better job of making content findable, searchable and so forth. So that's more of the proactive side of things. But it's also creating content that answers tough questions, such as, "Why do we need to slow down in the construction zone if there are no workers there?" You know how many people ask that question? A lot!

'So, we create content that answers those questions. Why do we close roads for eight hours? Because accidents are considered crime scenes. People don't understand the context sometimes. They just see, *I can get home*, or *I can't get home*. And I get it, that's their world, and that's all they care about, because it's what impacts them. To provide that context is really helpful when it comes to follow-up. Content we created seven years ago is still as relevant today because we created it for evergreen purposes. When we create it, like, "Hey, do we have a blog?" "Oh yeah, we wrote that in 2015. It's still useful. Yeah, we'll update it a little bit and then share it." Our focus is very much answering questions within a timeframe through Twitter, Facebook, Instagram. We also are on Flickr—yeah, Flickr still lives—and YouTube as well. We're using those platforms, Instagram Stories and so forth, to answer questions. That's the whole point, is to just get that engagement of, "Do you have questions? We have answers."'

Russel Lolacher is an advocate for great work relationships (EX and CX); a communication and engagement leader; a podcaster, speaker and continuous learner; and an ICMI Top 25 and CX Thought Leader. He is currently the director of digital communications (content, engagement, social) at the British Columbia Ministry of Transportation in Canada.

Pandemic communications case studies

If the pandemic expedited government and public sector's digital agility, what long-term tactics are here to stay? I spoke to a number of frontline communications professionals who shared their experiences and post-pandemic practices.

World Health Organization:
7 social media communications takeaways

The World Health Organization led the global public health communications effort throughout the pandemic. As a relatively small department, it's hard to understand how these experts had the capacity to scale messaging globally. But it was their shrewdness and strategic approach that supported their own communications as well as providing resources to national health agencies across the world.

For most of 2020 and 2021 they were the number one brand on social media. This lived experience on the pandemic frontline of communications means that they have vast experience to share.

Speaking at our 2021 Public Sector Digital Marketing Summit, WHO social media manager Aleksandra Kuzmanovic outlined her seven key takeaways from leading social media during a pandemic.

1. **Always be honest:** The public want to know the truth and expect to be told the truth in the public interest. Be known for being honest and you will build a loyal following of advocates who will share your posts.

2. **Work with your leadership:** Those leading from the front of the pandemic response, or any crisis, need support to solve operational and communications challenges, so work with your leadership to get their messages out quickly and broadly. Be sure to provide coaching and counselling to build up their confidence and competence if they are new to live social.

3. **Embrace team growth and skills:** Your team is critical to social media success, from topic experts to technical support and management. Involve everyone where appropriate and also work

closely within your own communications team, because this trust is what will keep your momentum up during the tough days. You should also upskill as you are developing new strategies because social media does not stand still.

4. **Follow your followers' needs:** Do not make assumptions that you know what your followers need. Lean into the data to understand their questions, concerns, misinformation and potential challenges to public health campaigns. Your followers and the insights from each channel should be guiding lights for your social communications strategy.

5. **Be out there and innovate:** Developing a high public profile for your organisation and your senior leaders and expert sources requires constant innovation, especially on social media, so lean into new innovations within social networks.

6. **Be timely:** Real-time information is the expectation of the public and during a pandemic the public health situation is changing daily, so being proactive with your social communications is key.

7. **Fight the infodemic with any tool at your disposal:** Collaborate with experts and partners to inform the public with trusted information. Staying silent is contributing to the fake news chaos.

WHO social communications innovations

Throughout the pandemic, the WHO social media team were innovating on social media. Here are some of the top tactics they introduced.

- Facebook Messenger and WhatsApp chatbot that provided real-time and country breakdowns of daily coronavirus case numbers along with public health guidance.

- Partnered with TikTok to create an informational page that provided trustworthy information, offered tips on staying safe and preventing the spread of the virus and dispelled myths around COVID-19.

- Multi-channel livestreams of press conferences and regular hosting of live Q&A sessions with public health experts.

- Building high profiles for the WHO senior leadership team to deepen public connection with the people behind the organisation. These senior leaders had frequent appearances across all social networks and shared tailored messages for audiences specific to each channel.

Health Service Executive, Ireland: social customer service

Ireland's health service provided social customer service with care and compassion—but how?

A single Tweet on March 14, 2020, marked the beginning of a two-year crisis that plunged Ireland into a public health emergency. Many of the country's five million citizens were about to experience life in a pandemic for the first time. It was a global event that was neither predicted nor expected.

Pandemic communications is a specialist skill that is earned on the frontline. In this case study we explore how Ireland's national health service, the Health Service Executive (HSE) responded to the public health emergency, developing coping mechanisms internally while providing service users with factual information on how they could protect themselves against the 2019 novel coronavirus.

In particular, let's explore the role of social media as part of the integrated communications strategy adopted by the HSE.

Much like the trajectory of the pandemic, the HSE's communications response came in waves, never stabilising long enough for staff to get a reprieve. Instead, the waves were like punctuation marks in the timelines of COVID-19 from early public health advice, to developing best practices, mask-wearing, testing and tracing, app downloads, vaccinations and boosters.

When the pandemic struck the HSE had a developed social media strategy and an active online presence. It also had experience in the game of public health crisis communications.

Twitter as an aid for corporate communications

Twitter was the first social network adopted by the HSE in August 2009 as a way of communicating real-time information about swine flu (H1N1), which had entered Ireland in May of that year.

The HSE realised the value of Twitter as a broadcast tool to alert the public to real-time updates of disruptions during major weather events; it was a valuable public relations tool to engage media; and it was central to public health campaigns. But Twitter became something much more than a broadcasting channel during 2020, 2021 and in 2022. It is now a dedicated customer service channel.

It was also the first social network that the HSE used to communicate and alert the public that Ireland had its first case of coronavirus in January 2020. Then the floodgates opened and the crisis communications plan for the novel coronavirus, as it was described in the early days, were well and truly open.

Social customer service is real public service

One of the glaring gaps in capacity was quickly exposed to the social media team when the Irish public sought real-time, trusted health advice. As the Taoiseach broadcast into every living room in the country, the public were dual-screening and going directly to HSE.ie.

In the years leading up to this pandemic the HSE made a deliberate decision to be the country's number one trusted health resource with radio advertisements broadcasting their tagline, *'Your number one trusted health website in Ireland. Brought to you by the Government of Ireland.'* You see the HSE were already in the business of building trust and this digital legwork paid off by early 2020.

With that trust came demand.

There was now a public appetite to ask Ireland's number one trusted source direct questions about these new health restrictions.

- How far should I social distance?
- How do I wash my hands properly?
- How do I wear a mask properly?
- Am I eligible for a vaccine?
- What are symptoms of COVID-19?

The list goes on.

Such was their tenacity to respond that they created a social customer service nightmare.

Ben Cloney, the HSE head of digital, said, 'We had a deep understanding of, and strategies for, great social media communications, but we were under-resourced for the scale and duration of the pandemic. A 9-to-5, Monday to Friday service had to transform into a 15-hour-a-day service, seven days a week. Our social channels shifted from "pushing" information to the public to conversing with them directly. It's about the 360-degree view of the citizen/public and being where they want us to be as opposed to forcing them to access information.' The HSE social team managed 170,000 DM queries from the Irish public during the pandemic and Social CX is now well and truly embedded into their social media strategy.

UK Government: livestreaming for public trust and transparency

The UK Government embraced livestreaming during the pandemic with frequent press conferences used to keep not only journalists updated, but also the public.

A traditional tool of public relations, media briefings have become a staple of social media content throughout the pandemic. UK citizens watched on as Prime Minister Boris Johnson and Chief Medical Officer professor Chris Whitty showed up on newsfeeds on Facebook and Twitter.

This display of public engagement bodes well for establishing real-time facts and dispelling myths. Livestreams are also available as replay videos and provide rich-media content for news websites.

The public comments under Facebook and Twitter livestreams appeared in the thousands, and while not all were in agreement with public health policy, they provided the press and communications teams with valuable insights into what the public felt, thought and intended to do about testing, contact tracing and vaccines.

Journalists watching on from the comfort of their kitchen tables were able to Zoom into these virtual events and so acted as a great aid for their work. This development has continued and the UK Government continue to broadcast live on their social networks with non-pandemic updates. It is a communications feature that has remained in their social media toolkit.

Citizens Information Board:
communicating complex information online

Ireland's Citizens Information Board (CIB) provide a valuable public service. They provide information, advice and advocacy on social services in Ireland through a network of local Citizens Information Centres (CICs), the national phone service CIPS and the website citizensinformation.ie.

They are also responsible for information and advice on money and budgeting through the Money Advice and Budgeting Service (MABS). This service is available via the MABS national helpline, in locations nationwide, online at MABS.ie and on chat via WhatsApp.

Pre-COVID-19 the organisation was more orientated to broadcast communications, but overnight they became a significant player in pandemic communications.

Starting out on their social media journey they were active on Twitter and Facebook only. They had little social presence for MABS.

Their strategy was broadcasting and not engaging. They steered clear of engagement with followers, did not answer direct queries and posted once a day with posts drafted well in advance. They had a social media strategy drafted with long-term, conservative goals, limited resources and a fear of engaging with the public and the risks involved.

The impact of the COVID-19 pandemic on their face-to-face service was immediate.

CIB staff had to learn to work in a different way with the suspension of face-to-face services across CIB and MABS. People were looking for information online, especially on social media. Misinformation had spread and there was a lack of reliable sources to counter this. But the Citizens Information Digital Content team and MABS Communications team in CIB were able to quickly pivot; the need to get this information out to the public was recognised—with social media identified as a key way to do this.

Their response to public demand was also immediate. The Citizens Information Board did the following:

- Resourced social media and set up a team to work on social

- Increased the number of posts and real-time updates with detailed, accessible information

- Responded to queries on social media

- Harnessed the power of Facebook, which they had recently set up

- Simplified their internal verification process, allowing for quicker responses

- Provided help when we the public needed it and leveraged the Citizens Information Phone Service

- Developed their own 'tone' and focused on consistency, speaking directly to the end user ('you')

- Promoted available local services

Citizens Information became a trusted source of information on social media and in fact their Tweets were added to Twitter's COVID-19 timeline and Facebook's COVID-19 Information Center.

Internally, they also had results:

- Broke down silos within the organisation, allowing increased collaboration and a better service for the users

- Improved their processes and leveraged tools such as SharePoint, Agorapulse, daily website updates, Canva

- Leaned into video content

- Increased buy-in from the organisation and engaging with citizens where they are (not just broadcasting to them)

The public service impact was clear.

CIB proved once again they are a meaningful source of truth, support, money and budgeting advice to a public in complete disarray. They provided an alternative way for citizens to engage with the advice available in a time of uncertainty, and the results demonstrate this:

- 23% increase in users to MABS.ie (March–October 2019)

- 8.46% increase in pageviews

- 25,145 blog pageviews with an average dwell of 3 minutes and 51 seconds

- 1,189 total conversations on chat (March–December 2019)

Bobby Barbour, MABS communications manager at CIB, says the lessons learned were so valuable and there is much that will continue. His advice is:

- **Keep what works:** Don't throw away what worked well during the pandemic.

- **Keep promoting social media and encouraging its growth:** It's not just an emergency response.

- **Focus on collaboration:** Tap into your people and trust your team.

- **Don't be afraid:** Be brave and answer people's queries on social.

- **It doesn't have to be perfect:** It is more important that you meet people's needs. Consider the three Cs: citizen-centred communications, content that drives conversation and consistency in your presence.

Department of Justice: hidden impact of domestic violence

If COVID-19 resulted in a public health pandemic, it also uncovered another epidemic: domestic violence. The award-winning Still Here campaign rolled out by Ireland's Department of Justice was in direct response to the escalating crisis behind closed doors in communities across the country. The rise in incidences and reports of domestic violence was a tragic and damaging consequence of isolation and lockdown during the first wave of the virus.

This case study illustrates that the power and importance of communications is key in very sensitive matters within society. Darragh Brennan, head of communications, says that the campaign was driven by data insights.

Collaboration was key in this campaign and as Brennan says, 'Government has the power of convening key stakeholders, bringing them to the table, to make decisions and take appropriate action.'

The campaign had two key objectives:

1. Ensure victims of domestic abuse knew where to access support services and ensure an increase in the number of calls to helplines by at least 15% during the duration of the campaign.

2. Ensure victims and the general public knew that domestic abuse support services were still available with a target of over 75% recall and awareness of the Still Here campaign message.

The campaign message was clear and it spoke to victims who were too afraid to speak up, but based on the research, it proved to have a

significant emotional connection which ultimately led to more victims picking up the phone to Women's Aid and asking for help.

'If your home isn't safe, support is still here.'

Social media and mainstream media campaigns directed victims
to ask for help and a dedicated landing page on gov.ie was set up. A
county-by-county directory of supports was published with immediate access via smartphone.

This campaign reached thousands of victims on social media and
provided a link to supports in a confidential way.

The campaign video on YouTube had over half a million views
and almost 23,000 website views. Just under 9 in 10 people surveyed could recall something about domestic violence supports still
being available during the COVID-19 crisis, while 4 in 5 deemed the
campaign effective in letting people know where they needed to go
if they required help or advice relating to domestic violence during
the pandemic.

All frontline services reported a significant increase in the number of people contacting their helplines during the campaign. The
stakeholders attributed this increase to the impact of the communications campaign.

One national service outlined around a 40% increase in the number of people contacting them. Another cited over a 350% increase.
In addition to this, the stillhere.ie website received more than
20,000 hits during the campaign with people looking for information on localised services.

* * * * *

YOU CAN WATCH THESE case studies in full on the Public Sector
Marketing Show YouTube channel.

9

Crisis Management
in the Digital Age

How to take control of a PR crisis
that begins or escalates online

Throughout my 21 years working in communications, I have been on all sides of PR crises: reporting on them as a broadcast journalist, shielding my clients as a PR practitioner and now preventing and managing them online.

PR crises come in many guises and across all media formats. The disruption of media, the explosion of online content and the introduction of the citizen journalist voice provide new challenges for PR and media professionals working in government and public sector.

The role of the traditional PR manager has evolved into a digital media specialist. However, the core skills of communications professionals have never been more important. We need expert government officials to produce clear, true content in an age of incessant opinion and worrying fake news. PR crisis prevention is better than disaster management cure.

Social media, community and digital marketing managers do not always come with a PR or journalistic background, so it is important that your management team meets to discuss the potential for any

PR crisis on social media. You should be able to define what possible threats pose damage to your organisation and have a plan to deal with each—from announcing job losses to white collar crime, workplace accidents, technology failures or cyber-bullying.

External factors—from cyber-attacks to terrorism, economic crashes to political turmoil—are beyond your control, but choosing how you react can give you some of that control back. Being prepared for a digital PR crisis will help mitigate the damage to brand and organisational trust, and should be prioritised like any other function in your organisation.

It is inevitable that any PR crisis will escalate on social media. It does not matter whether you believe the opinions or not—trust is the currency of public interest messaging. News desks are watching social media and taking the public temperature of topics on Facebook and Twitter, which is influencing editorial decisions.

To highlight how a traditional skillset can be adapted in the age of social media, what follows is my own formula for how to put out a PR fire that ignites on social media. Because when the chips are down, you need to rise up.

The Crisis Communications Probability Matrix©

In order to be adequately prepared, you need to be able to establish the possible crises that may arise. Before writing your crisis communications plan, you should craft a Crisis Communications Probability Matrix© that is specific to your organisation. I have developed this method aimed at giving you foresight, instead of waiting on a good crisis to give you hindsight.

The Crisis Communications Probability Matrix© formula

There are five steps you need to take when developing a crisis action plan:

1. Establish examples of **types of crises** that may impact your department/organisation.

2. Categorise each crisis by type: either as **'internal'** or **'external'** (these are marked by 'I' and 'E' in the sample plan that follows).

3. Decide what **expertise** you will need for each particular crisis. Remember, this may include outside expertise.

4. Detail the **fallout** and impact of each possible crisis on your department/organisation.

5. Define who the crisis is going to impact most by listing the **audiences** in the firing line.

Here are a few examples of how this preparation might look:

CRISIS	TYPE	EXPERTISE	FALLOUT	AUDIENCE
Workplace accident	I	CEO, Health & Safety officer, Head of Communications, external advisor	Death or serious injury, criminal or civil proceedings, dismissal, fines, reputation damage, negative online reviews, reduced public confidence, negative social media commentary	Staff member/s, family, colleagues, sister companies, industry body, customers, suppliers, media, public
Cyber-attack	E	CEO, CIO, IT senior, Department Head, Head of Communications, external advisor	Compromise private data, compromise IT systems, breakdown in internal & external communications, reputation damage, financial loss, share price fall, civil proceedings, negative online reviews, reduced public confidence, negative social media commentary	Staff, customers, industry body, suppliers, media, public
Customer complaint	E	CEO, Head of Customer Service, Department Head, Head of Communications, external advisor	Negative online reviews, loss of trade, reputation damage, cost of increased marketing spend, reduced public confidence, decrease in online community numbers (social, email subscribers), negative social media commentary	Customer, staff, online community, suppliers, public
Product recall	E	Chairman of Board, CEO, Head of Product Development, Head of R&D, Head of Health & Safety, Head of Communications, external advisor	Substantial financial losses due to product recall, increased spend on marketing communications, loss of distributors, customer confidence, reduced customer base, share price fall, reputation damage, negative online sentiment, loss of product/trading licence	Customers, distributors, suppliers, industry body, media, public

CRISIS	TYPE	EXPERTISE	FALLOUT	AUDIENCE
White collar crime	I	Chairman of Board, CEO, CFO, Head of Communications, Governance Director, private investigator, external advisor	Reputation damage, dis-engaged staff, fall in share price, negative online commentary, public anger at individual/s and/or company	Board of Directors, staff, suppliers, public, media, law enforcement
Media leak of sensitive information	I	Chairman of Board, CEO, Deputy CEO, Head of Department, Governance Director, Head of Communications, external advisor	Extensive negative PR across traditional and online media, distraction and time-consuming from day-to-day operations, fall in share price, loss of customers, data protection issues	Board of Directors, staff, suppliers, media, public
Financial crisis	I	Chairman of Board, CEO, CFO, Head of Communications, external advisor	Company losses, share price fall, job losses, restructuring, reloca-tion, company closure	Board of Directors, staff, suppliers, media, public
Job losses	I	CEO, Head of HR, Head of Communications external advisor	Staff anger, union negotiations, negative public opinion, staff sit-in, staff protests, negative social media commentary	Board of Directors, staff, union, media, suppliers, public
High-profile resignation	I	Chairman of Board, CEO, Head of HR, Head of Communications, external advisor	Public arguments among resigning staff members and management, public questioning and commentary, media investi-gations, share price fall, discord among management	Board of Directors, staff, media, suppliers, public
Organisation closure	I	Chairman of Board, CEO, CFO, Head of Communications, external advisor	Union negotiations, negative media commentary in traditional and online media, negative social commentary, staff publicly commenting, industry investi-gation, reputation damage for company and key individuals, disgruntled suppliers not paid	Boards of Directors, shareholders, staff, suppliers, union, media, public
Internal whistleblower revelations	I	Chairman of Board, CEO, Head of Communications, Head of Department, external advisor	Extensive negative and prolonged media coverage, industry inves-tigation, suspension of staff, internal investigation, reputation damage, negative social media commentary, uncovering of further matters leading to more whistleblowers, criminal or civil proceedings, company losses, company restructuring, resigna-tions, share price fall, company closure	Boards of Directors, staff, suppliers, union, industry body, media, public

CRISIS	TYPE	EXPERTISE	FALLOUT	AUDIENCE
Personal information of staff indirectly impacting organisation	I	Chairman of Board, CEO, Head of Communications, Head of HR, external advisor	Staff speculation and discord, media door-stepping, reputation damage, negative social media commentary, share price fall, loss of customers, resignations	Board of Directors, shareholders, staff, suppliers, staff members' family, media, public
Media exposé	E	Chairman of Board, CEO, Head of Communications, Head of Department, external advisor	Extensive negative and prolonged media coverage, industry investigation, staff speculation and discord, media door-stepping, reputation damage, negative social media commentary, share price fall, loss of customers, resignations	Board of Directors, staff, suppliers, media, public
Firing of senior staff member	I	Chairman of Board, CEO, Head of Communications, Head of Department, external advisor	Extensive negative and prolonged media coverage, industry investigation, staff speculation and discord, media door-stepping, public debate between company and staff member in questions, reputation damage, negative social media commentary, share price fall, loss of customers, resignations	Board of Directors, staff, suppliers, media, public
Natural disaster	E	Chairman of Board, CEO, CIO, COO, Head of Communications, Emergency Planning Team, external advisor	Staff injuries or death, loss of infrastructure/buildings, financial loss, loss of stock, share price fall, closure of company for a time or permanently, long-term impact on staff health, negative social media commentary	Law enforcement, emergency services, local authority, Board of Directors, staff, suppliers, media, public
Terrorist attack	E	Chairman of Board, CEO, CIO, COO, Head of Communications, Emergency Planning Team, external advisor	Staff injuries or death, loss of infrastructure/buildings, financial loss, loss of stock, share price fall, closure of company for a time or permanently, long-term impact on staff health, negative social media commentary	Law enforcement, emergency services, local authority, Board of Directors, staff, suppliers, media, public
Governance practices	I	Chairman of Board, CEO, CIO, COO, CFO, Head of Communications, Governance Director, external advisor	Civil or criminal proceedings, losing trading or product licence, resignations, expulsion of staff members, leading to whistle-blowers going to the media, share price fall, loss of customers, restructuring, investment in new practices, technology and/or systems, investment in new training programmes, negative social media commentary	Board of Directors, staff, industry body, suppliers, media, public

CRISIS	TYPE	EXPERTISE	FALLOUT	AUDIENCE
Systems/ service/ technology failure	I	Chairman of Board, CEO, CIO, COO, CFO, Head of Communications, external advisor	Civil or criminal proceedings, loss of trading time, share price fall, loss of customers, investment in new technology and/ or systems, investment in new training programmes, negative social media commentary	Board of Directors, staff, industry body, suppliers, media, public
Workplace violence: bullying, harassment, sexual assault, physical assault	I	Chairman of Board, CEO, Head of HR, Head of Communications, external advisor	Resignations, expulsion of staff members, police investigation, civil or criminal proceedings, share price fall, loss of customers, negative social media commentary	Law enforcement, Board of Directors, staff, industry body, suppliers, media, public
Cyber-bullying	E	Chairman of Board, CEO, Head of HR, Head of Communications, external advisor	Resignations, expulsion of staff members, police investigation, civil or criminal proceedings, share price fall, loss of customers, negative social media commentary	Law enforcement, Board of Directors, staff, industry body, suppliers, media, public
Political crisis, legislative changes	E	Chairman of Board, CEO, CIO, COO, CFO, Head of Communications, external advisor	Share price fall, need to relocate to new region/territory/country, cost of doing business increases, loss of senior staff, market and company uncertainty	Board of Directors, staff, industry body, sister companies in other regions, suppliers, media, public

Developing an online crisis management (OCM) team

Crisis communications requires a skillset to manage the media and public simultaneously. Ensure the right people are at the table when making preparatory key decisions and when you are in response mode. Everyone should be clear on their roles and responsibilities.

What follows are the roles that need to be filled by a mix of staff in your department or organisation. What is most important is their skillset. You may find that some or most of these roles do not exist in your organisation. In this case, you might consider how you might fill the gaps, for example, with external consultants or subject matter experts.

- **Chair of OCM team:** Requests and hosts crisis meetings; role could be filled by the CEO, director or communications director.

- **Spokesperson:** The face and voice of the crisis who will speak to the media and directly to the public (via social media).

- **PR manager:** Directing the official media statements and briefing spokesperson for media interviews.

- **Specialist:** An individual with specialised knowledge on the topic of the crisis; they might be an external advisor.

- **Social media manager:** The head of social media, who will either be a skilled community manager or will be directing their team on community management and scheduling live broadcasts.

- **Head of department:** If the crisis affects a specific department, the head of department needs to be at the table; involve them from the start.

- **Web manager:** The person responsible for updating the website and sharing real-time emergency response information.

- **Data analyst:** The team member responsible for analysing your web and social data, as well as setting up and monitoring social listening.

- **Customer service director:** If you have a customer service call centre, it is advisable to have the head of operations attend.

- **Health and safety manager:** Depending on the crisis, you may need your health and safety manager in attendance.

One person must be responsible for taking the minutes and signing off on the agreed actions. The minute-taker will then need to communicate those agreed actions to the relevant staff, with clear guidance on what is expected of them in terms of deliverables and timeframes.

OCM team meetings should take place frequently until the crisis is resolved. In the first 24 hours, the team may even sit throughout the night, depending on the nature of the emergency.

Setting Internal Policies

WHEN A PR crisis hits, the social media rocket is going to take off. You can choose to be inside the capsule steering the direction of its flight, or standing on the platform as a spectator.

Ask yourself and senior management these three questions:

- What **policies** are in place in terms of crisis management? (For example, social listening policy, escalation policy, crisis management policy.)

- Do existing policies **support** potential crises?

- Have your senior staff been **trained** in how to use their personal profiles during a crisis? If not, can this instruction (sometimes referred to as a Digital Citizenship programme) be incorporated into your ongoing internal training?

The PAR cycle online crisis response (preparation, action and reaction)

The following practical steps will not only help you deal with a crisis internally and externally, they can actually help prevent a crisis from happening if you practice them consistently on an ongoing basis. When developing these steps for your organisation, include specifics relating to your own action plan, including response times, statements, actions to take, live monitoring of the situation and the expertise, fallout and audiences you outlined previously in your Crisis Communications Probability Matrix©.

THE PAR CYCLE

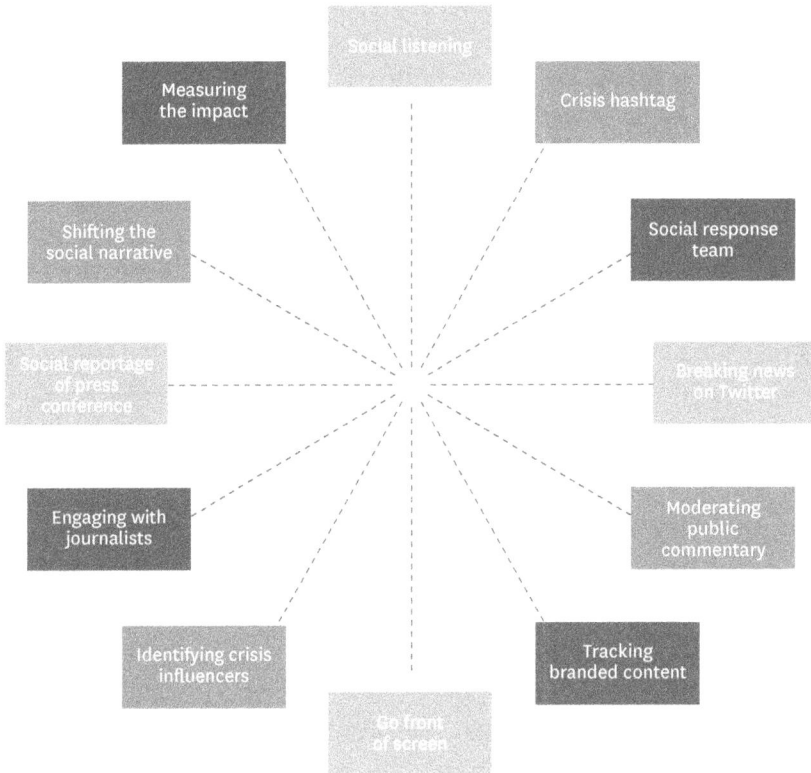

- **Social listening:** You need to immediately set up tracking of the main keywords, phrases and names associated with the crisis.

- **Crisis hashtag:** Create your own crisis hashtag, or use a trending one. If the trending one is negative, you may consider creating a positive one.

- **Social response team:** Hold your first meeting and get together as soon as possible.

- **Breaking news on Twitter:** Keep an eye on breaking news and provide real-time updates on Twitter. Use Twitter threads, Twitter Spaces and Twitter Live to best advantage.

- **Moderating public commentary:** Have a team member watch the public conversation, which can help direct the PR and media strategy.

- **Tracking branded content:** Monitor all mentions of your brand and key individuals across the web and social media.

- **Go front of screen:** Don't forget to use video as your storytelling ally and be brave enough to go front of screen.

- **Identifying crisis influencers:** Who are the voices that are holding the most share of social voice in this crisis? Are they against or supporting you?

- **Engaging with journalists:** Stay in touch with journalists via Twitter and on the phone, and use them to correct the record if fake news is being shared online.

- **Social reportage of press conference:** If you are hosting a media briefing or press conference, be sure to livestream it on social media. See chapter 7 for more on how to livestream.

- **Shifting the social narrative:** Answer all the public's concerns (which you pick up from social listening) and ask key influencers and experts to step into the social media conversations. Remember, you need to have maximum share of voice online to sway public opinion.

- **Measuring the impact:** Your data analyst and media team need to provide regular reports on the sentiment, extent of media coverage and public commentary around the crisis.

The 1524 Action Plan

Even when you follow all the steps of the PAR cycle and have proactive policies in place, crises are likely to happen. If and when they do, immediate action is critical to effectively restrict the impact. Within the first 24 hours of a crisis event, there are 15 actions you need to take. My 1524 Action Plan can act as a road map for those steps in those first critical hours.

1. Establish the facts

It is important to be clear on the facts, as you will be communicating these in a timely manner to the traditional media and also on your website and social networks. External communications should only happen when internal stakeholders and key players are informed first. Consider the following questions, remembering that timing is everything:

- **What** is the crisis?
- **Who** is involved?
- **How** did it happen?
- **Where** did it happen?
- **Why** did it happen?
- **When** did it happen?

2. From golden hour to golden moments

Before the arrival of social media, the PR professional worked a crisis based on the 'The Golden Hour'. Consider how much content is shared on the social web in just 60 minutes. You need to be able to direct the narrative and be in the communications driving seat.

3. 'No comment' is not an option

What do you think when you hear the words 'no comment'? Yes, me too. We immediately think: 'What do they have to hide?' or 'There's no smoke without fire.' Don't let doubt seep into social media. The media will always find their story and, whether you comment or not, they will report on your crisis. And citizen journalists are also contributing to and shaping the narrative.

4. Monitor your brand across all media types

If you are not doing so already, set up online brand monitoring for your organisation and key people, topic keywords associated with the crisis and names of anyone else involved. By monitoring your brand during a PR crisis, you can react in real time while gauging online sentiment. This will also help you prepare for media interviews.

Assessing the Severity of a Crisis

ONCE YOU HAVE established the facts of a given crisis, define it in one of the following ways:

In the public interest, i.e., the public are directly affected and/or it is of direct concern to the public.

or

Of interest to the public, i.e., the public are not directly affected, but they have an interest in the crisis.

The next step is to establish the severity of the crisis, which can help you determine your response:

- **Extreme:** The crisis is a major incident involving multiple people and directly impacting staff or public safety.

- **Severe:** The crisis is isolated to one site and is contained but there is a risk it may impact student, staff or public safety.

- **High:** The crisis has a major impact on the entire organisation but will not impact student, staff or public safety.

- **Medium:** The crisis is internal, contained and relates to an administrative, systems or technological failure.

- **Low:** The crisis is isolated to one office and can be resolved with relative ease.

5. Prepare your statement

A media statement is an invaluable part of your communications crisis toolbox. It will establish the facts for the media, the public, your clients, staff and any other relevant stakeholders. If the facts are not publicly shared, then there is a silo of opportunity for rumour and hearsay to gather momentum. You want to prevent this at all costs. You will want to have a landing page or live blog on your website that is updated as public announcements are made. Sign-post social conversations to this link.

6. Brief internal stakeholders first

Before you brief the media, brief internal stakeholders, for example, heads of department, government minister and staff. You can give them a short outline of the crisis and what action you are taking. This can be a shorter version of the media statement or a copy of it. Just leave a five-minute gap between internal and external release.

7. Media engagement

You should have an up-to-date media list on file at all times. If you do not have one already, you can create one by calling the main media outlets and getting the contact details of the relevant reporter. Do not send your press release to the general news desk email address. Once engaged in conversations with the media, there are appropriate ways to manage that relationship.

8. One face, one voice

The media will want to speak to a representative about the crisis. Don't expect to issue a media statement and refuse to speak to the media in person. When you are ready to speak to the media it is vital that you identify one spokesperson who will do all media interviews throughout the crisis process (the Crisis Communications Probability Matrix© on page 162 can help you choose the right spokesperson for the situation). This consistency of face and voice is critical. They must be an impressive media performer, knowledgeable of the facts and all updates and be able to instil confidence. Consider the role of social and live video for breaking and ongoing updates.

9. Prepare the nasty questions

Brainstorm the top 10 nasty questions that you possibly could be asked by a reporter and prepare answers to each. While undertaking this task, ensure you include questions that you do not believe should be asked. You have to think like a journalist in this instance.

Keep a matrix of FNCs (frequent nasty comments) and ask management to provide answers to these comments so that the community manager has positions and answers to provide where appropriate. Your FNC matrix should be a live document (a Google Doc works well) and the community manager should be responsible for keeping it updated and seeking out the responses. They are not responsible for providing the answers—this needs to be done by the relevant manager or expert.

Here is an example of how that matrix could look:

COMMENT	CHANNEL	ANSWER
Write the nasty comment	Identify which channel	The language should reflect the channel provided, and keep your crisis policy and organisation's objectives in mind

10. Be social media ready

Simultaneously share your press release on your website and across your social networks, repurposing the content of the statement for each channel. Do not wait for the media to Tweet it out. Your social media manager should be involved in all PR crisis meetings and have the experience to deal with community engagement around your crisis. Pull back or delete any pre-scheduled content on social—the tone or timing may be wrong. Leverage social and live video to control the story.

11. Turn a crisis into an opportunity

If you plan for a crisis, have an open and transparent approach, use a well-briefed and competent spokesperson, accept any wrongdoing or faults and take action early, then the crisis could in fact showcase your spokesperson as one that is transparent and trustworthy. Don't waste a good crisis!

12. Shift public opinion

Identify which beliefs you need to shift and why. The role of individual senior leaders on social media is important to achieve this. Having multiple authoritative and expert voices will ensure the public are getting reliable and trusted information from multiple sources.

Even as a given crisis subsides, the final three steps of the 1524 Action Plan can help you improve your response to future crises:

13. Learn lessons

With any crisis, there are many valuable lessons to be learned. It is incumbent on the organisation to sit down and reflect on the crisis and its impact on all stakeholders and not just to silence the media or public. Morale, trust, reputational and long-term organisational damage may have been inflicted. Identify a person or a team to draft a report on lessons learnt and how to avoid a similar crisis in the future.

14. PR evaluation of crisis

A full evaluation of the crisis from a public relations and social media perspective must be undertaken shortly after it has abated. Identify a person or a team to do this and ensure there are clear terms of reference given for this evaluation. Metrics should include sentiment, share of voice, online public mentions, hashtag reach, website traffic, social media growth/reduction, media mentions, most shared angles of the crisis and overall narrative evaluation.

15. Bespoke crisis communications SOP

From your PR evaluation of the crisis, you will be able to draw up a standard operating procedure (SOP) document. Recruit external expertise to review your digital PR crisis communications plan to see if it can be improved in any way. Brief all relevant staff on the new document and upskill any staff members who require training.

Trolling and online abuse

Online abuse is an almost inevitable reality when managing any online forums. Here are the steps you should take to prepare for it, and deal with it when it happens:

1. **Report all incidents.** Abusive, offensive, threatening or defamatory comments should be reported to the relevant social network.

2. **Block abusers.** Users who engage in this type of abusive commentary should be blocked from the relevant organisational social network. Screenshot the abuse as evidence before blocking.

3. **Involve the authorities if needed.** Serious threats made against an individual or an organisation on any of your social networks should be reported to the relevant authorities, including the police.

4. **Disable commenting if needed.** Consistent abusive commentary on social post threads may result in comments being disabled for that specific post.

5. **Use social listening.** You can't monitor all posts 24/7, so you need to employ social listening to catch any out-of-hour comments or posts of concern.

6. **State your policies.** Include your community management policy on your social networks or a link to them, and ask your community to respect others' comments on your account, as abuse will not be tolerated.

7. **Involve the relevant teams.** Queries or comments relating to organisational services should be dealt with by the relevant citizen service teams, and media queries sent to your press team.

8. **Offer clear guidelines for your users.** Encourage your users not to share personal information on your social networks.

9. **Include emergency contacts.** If you are a frontline emergency provider, include the emergency call line number in your bio.

10. **Go one-on-one when needed.** Advise users to speak privately to your organisation using Direct Message on Twitter, Private Message on Facebook, via email or through phone calls, which the community manager can then escalate and sign-post to the relevant expert or manager.

11. **Encourage reporting.** Advise followers who may be concerned about any content posted on any of your social networks by you, or by a third party, to report it to a specific email address.

12. **Have a complaints policy.** And link to that policy with a URL to a landing page.

Escalating concerns

All incidents of online abuse should have an escalation protocol. Here is how the steps in such a protocol could look:

1. Screenshot particular social media message.
2. Share with social media manager (who may escalate it further).
3. Take action to publicly respond to individual, either to correct the record or sign-post them until there is further information (all incidents to be reviewed on their own merit).
4. Take action to hide comment.
5. Take action to remove and block individual.
6. If blocked, report individual to relevant social network.
7. Raise at weekly digital communications meeting once it has been dealt with.
8. Document it as a Social Media Abuse Incident (SMAI) and save on file.

Preparing for social media and public sector policy dilemmas

When policy dilemmas take centre stage, it can be incredibly difficult to know what to post on social media, as they will be publicly divisive and saying nothing might feel like the best option. Knowing how to manage social media communications in all scenarios, however, is an important part of your social media strategy.

These two steps can help you prepare, so that you can navigate these dilemmas efficiently when they arise:

1. Take part in the conversation

Your department can't afford to be absent from discussion about policies that are relevant to your citizens, even if you know they are going to cause massive furore online. Open a dialogue on your accounts that will allow you to correct mistakes and establish truth, as well as give you a better idea of what citizens genuinely want from you. Asking the public for their feedback is a great way to start off.

2. Set standards for your social networks

While you want to give all of your followers a voice, there's a point at which you need to remove comments from your accounts. For example, you might want to remove comments that are filled with profanity or that deliberately attack another member of your community. As a government agency, keeping up with your social media page is a critical part of ensuring that your citizens have all the information they need—and will help you build trust and transparency for your office. Add in profanity filters which will prevent comments with particular words or phrases from appearing on your accounts.

The final report

At the end of any crisis, prepare a report for senior leaders on the crisis response, outcome and learnings. Your report should include:

- A summary of the specific crisis.
- An overview of your metrics, including social mention stats, reach of crisis topic/hashtag, key influencers, sentiment, social reach and engagement and online media mentions.

- All of the main social channels that were involved and the one that dominated.
- Who was on the response team.
- What the response messages were.
- What response actions were taken.
- The learnings you have taken from the crisis.
- Any updates to policies and protocols that might be required.
- Any other relevant matters.

* * * * *

IT IS COMMON FOR PR crises to begin on social media and turn into a firestorm within minutes. This crisis-in-waiting requires public sector bodies to have a robust plan of action in place. We have no choice but to put a sharp focus on S3 Age crisis management. Pre-digital, we had to concern ourselves with the media fallout from a PR meltdown, but today we have a whole host of other challenges, not least public commentary on social media. The adage *fail to prepare, prepare to fail* is appropriate here.

How social media can save lives

It may seem far-fetched to suggest that social media can save lives, but it is proven to be an invaluable tool for law enforcement agencies and frontline responders in managing and directing emergency response.

We now live in a world that is effectively an online global village. The sophistication of smartphones and the growth in social networking sites empowers members of the public to connect with like-minded people with shared interests, whether they are innocent or darker interests.

Much of the conversations online produce publicly available data; combined with technology, this data allows for social monitoring. The behaviour of having open privacy settings on social networking sites is commonplace worldwide, and has led to a situation where the general public are now providing law enforcement agencies with more personal information than ever before—and most people are probably providing more than they even realise. But while the downsides of this widespread privacy issue could be debated, such an availability of information has a clear upside for emergency response agencies.

Social media can step up in emergency situations. Frontline responders, especially police agencies, can reach a large audience quickly, establish what is known in the public domain (true or untrue), manage the information they put out and do all of this with a sense of immediacy and confidence, often from one dashboard or screen from a centralised control room.

Of the 4.5 billion social media users, 99% access their accounts via their mobile phone. This means that citizens are both accessing and sharing information on the go and capturing real-life, real-time incidents, which in turn is accessed by emergency responders. Social media gives the public an opportunity to be an extension of an emergency response team, before, during and after a public disaster.

We are all very well aware that with social media comes the 'big brother' effect. The social web allows for deep data mining and monitoring of individual accounts and big data. We all accept that social media is here to stay, but the rise in social media use is making it more and more difficult for emergency response agencies to 'hear' meaningful social conversations that will contribute to their response duties.

In the context of law enforcement agencies, for example, there are a myriad of reasons as to why you would want to use monitoring technologies. These include:

- Establishing sentiment towards the police force among its citizens.
- Predicting potential fractious protests or events.
- Measuring engagement on a particular public information campaign.
- Identifying or monitoring persons of interest in a criminal investigation.
- Engaging the public's support.
- Tracking incidences of cyber-crime.
- Monitoring cyber-warfare or identifying hot beds of incitement to hatred or war.

When it comes to first-responder agencies' use of social media monitoring tools, the words of social media strategist and speaker Jay Baer come to mind: 'The end goal is action, not eyeballs.'

Officers or civilians working on social media strategies for first-responder agencies must harness the power of their online communities. Since the establishment of the very first police force, the citizen has been at the heart of law enforcement in terms of their power, and obligation, to report incidences of crime. Since we are now living in an online global village with the arrival of the digital revolution, the eyeballs of the digital citizen have so much more power. In the next few pages, I will show you how two different agencies in two different regions have used social media to improve their emergency response management.

The Dublin Fire Brigade

The Dublin Fire Brigade operates in Ireland's capital city, responding to over 30,000 fire and rescue incidents and more than 85,000 emergency ambulance incidents each year. They have 14 fire stations, with 1,000 staff members.

In creating a social media strategy for preparedness, the Dublin Fire Brigade decided on three pillars:

- **Prevent:** Educate their community on ways to prevent fires from starting, plus electrical safety, water safety, road safety and chemical safety.

- **Inform:** Alert the public to fires and accidents, and invite their followers to inform them of new fires or accidents.

- **Promote:** Show all the valuable ways the Fire Brigade helps its community on a daily basis.

  'There was recognition within Dublin Fire Brigade that we didn't really do anything to promote ourselves. So, we decided to use social media to change that.'

  RAY MCMONAGLE, firefighter/paramedic, Dublin Fire Brigade

Social media tactics

The Dublin Fire Brigade uses Twitter, Facebook, Instagram and Snapchat to post news and public safety messages around their **Prevent, Inform and Promote** strategy.

For **Prevent**, they post about the risks of overcharging your phone, dangerous electrical sockets and wires, staying safe near water, driving safely, Christmas lights safety, late-night cooking hazards and more.

For **Inform**, they share real-time incidents around the city and alert people to accidents they should avoid, while repeating messages around safety. They also clarify any false reports or fake news about fires in their jurisdiction.

For **Promote**, they tell personal stories, from showcasing open-house days and engaging with charities and local schools to new cadets completing training.

> 'The perception is that we simply put out fires, attend accidents and rescue cats. But we do a lot more than that and we want the public to see that.'
>
> RAY MCMONAGLE, firefighter/paramedic, Dublin Fire Brigade

The results

The results of their planned and engaging content are evident.

The Dublin Fire Brigade appeals to the public and tells them to stay safe, take a different route home from work, collect their kids from school (or not) during a major incident or even get their washing in before their clothes get smoke damaged.

But not only does their social content benefit the public, it also adds operational value to the fire service. This is done by keeping the public away from incidents, keeping them safe (indoors) and getting the public to help them by sending photos from incidents for intelligence purposes.

Also, because they can show the breadth of their services and give people access to what happens behind the scenes, they are able to be even more embedded and respected in their community.

'Our reactive messages, showing incidents where there was a lucky escape, like a mobile phone burning a carpet, are much more effective than a proactive safety post. People see and quickly understand the reality.'

RAY MCMONAGLE, firefighter/paramedic, Dublin Fire Brigade

Key takeaways

The Dublin Fire Brigade learned the lesson of needing a coherent content plan to make the most of their social media channels.

By starting with trial and error, they soon recognised the three pillars that would allow them to operate more effectively and build more trust within their communities.

They also knew that by engaging with the public in the right way, they would earn new followers, which they could in turn educate to stay safe and help prevent any further tragedies.

'Because we work behind cordons we're sometime seen as unapproachable, so our social media allows us to engage with the public in a more personable way, whether it's a fun, light post or a serious safety message.'

RAY MCMONAGLE, firefighter/paramedic, Dublin Fire Brigade

The Dublin Fire Brigade has developed the right balance between what they post, which channels they use and how they talk to the people they serve. They like Twitter best because of its fast-paced, real-time appeal, but they also can engage with less immediate information through Facebook, Instagram and Snapchat.

Their core pillars of Prevent, Inform and Promote have helped them develop a large base of followers, which allows for better collaboration with the public.

They also use the following approach to engage with their community on a daily basis:

- Be personable.
- Be friendly.

- Be honest and transparent.
- Listen to feedback.
- Don't be defensive.
- Revert to queries or concerns promptly.

The Arizona Police Department

Chris Adamczyk is a global threat intelligence specialist formerly with the social media analyst team at the Mesa Police Department in Arizona. For Chris, it is all about putting a robust communications plan in place prior to events and crises, like natural disasters, so the event's marketers or first responders can feed into it. Chris says a solid plan is important because the potential for danger is everywhere:

- Any large event can become a disaster.
- Any location can come under attack.
- Any storm can turn into a flood.

Chris says that, these days, even a marketing expert can save lives, by providing and promoting hashtags that people can use if they get into distress at major events.

Hashtags before phone calls

Chris says that people in a crisis situation are just as likely to Tweet a request for help as call the emergency services. People are increasingly using official event hashtags to call for help, before they even think of contacting the emergency services. So, in this case, it is up to emergency analysts to find out who needs help most by sifting through all the many posts, comments and shares surrounding the crisis. Chris used the examples of both Hurricane Harvey and Hurricane Irma, where #HarveyRescue or #IrmaSOS were used in the first real shift to social media as a distress call from the public during large-scale events.

This means that emergency response teams need to put new strategies in place to deal with the changing trends. While effective response seems obvious, Chris sees preparation as being more key, as getting this right means a much better response.

Tactics for being prepared

Here are the tactics Chris suggests emergency response teams employ at the planning stage:

1. *Know the lexicon of any event*

This can include things like the hashtags or keywords.

2. *Pull together the workflow plan*

This should be broken down in the following stages:

Discover—find the emergency
Verify—establish its authenticity
Attribute—categorise the type of response needed
Isolate—clarify the specific action that needs to be taken
Record—register the response with the responders
Act—ensure the response is carried out

3. *Prepare your means of communication*

This should be broken into three phases:

Analyst phase—have people searching for legitimate requests for help
Checkpoint phase—verify and categorise the help that is required
End user phase—communicate with the responders to act (fire brigade, ambulance, etc.)

4. *Prepare your communications team*

Ideally, this will involve three people:

Finder—this will be the person who will look after the analyst phase to sift through and find responses using the publicly available data from social networks and network analysis
Researcher—this will be the person who establishes the authenticity and proximity of the request for help

Manager—this is the overseer who will be in charge of getting the response teams to act and listen to their feedback

> 'In a crisis situation, you can't rely on luck alone. You've got to be fully prepared and ready to respond at any moment.'
>
> CHRIS ADAMCZYK, former social media intelligence analyst, Mesa Police Department, AZ

Responding effectively

Chris describes social media in a crisis situation as 'looking like digital hell in a hand basket.' With such potential for heightened emotion and confusion, it is your team's job to stick to the plan. He recommends the following approach:

- **Keep calm.** People may get animated, but it is your role to calmly execute the plan, and this is where good preparation will serve you well.

- **Stick to your workflow.** The plan is there because it works, so stick to it.

- **The plan is task orientated, not people orientated.** Don't get sidetracked by emotions or people who want you to veer away from the plan.

The social media newsroom for emergency responders

In working with groups like municipal authorities and police departments, I have created my own integrated social media management approach. I developed this model specifically for law enforcement agencies but in fact it can be used by any emergency response team around the world. This guide also includes advice for a number of individual departments.

The social media newsroom for emergency responders model has five areas of responsibility:

THE LAW ENFORCEMENT
SOCIAL MEDIA NEWSROOM

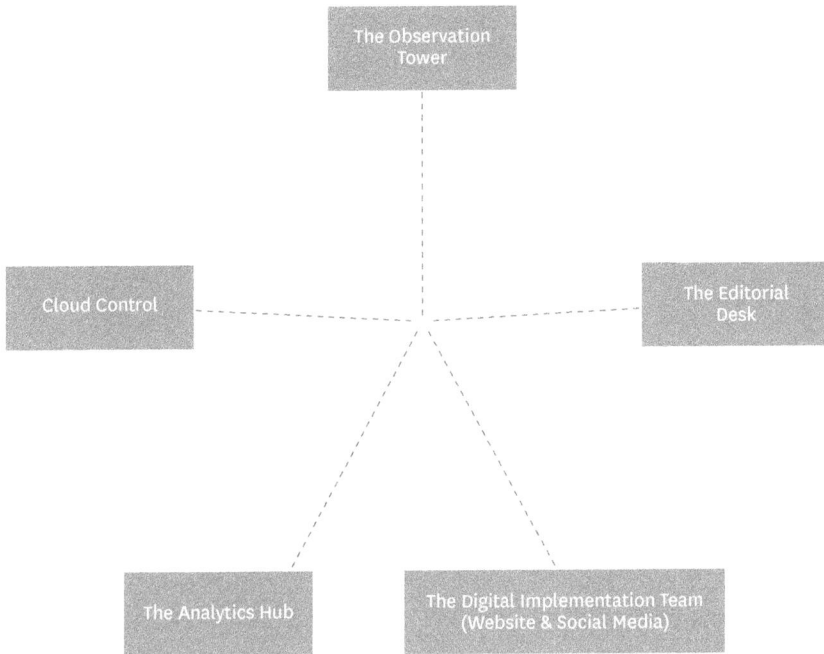

1. The Observation Tower

From the Observation Tower, senior communications managers develop the social media strategy, aligning it with the corporate and operational needs of the team.

The roles here include strategic planning, developing a social media use policy, evaluation and review of social media performance and the overall management of the department. The skills required include strategic digital marketing, and knowledge of and experience in corporate and communications policy with an acute awareness of communications in the specific field, e.g., law enforcement or emergency response communications.

2. The Editorial Desk

Within this department, the editor defines the content plan for the year, in terms of big campaigns and corporate messages, while also including the communications needs of each unit within the agency.

The role of the team includes strategic content planning and management, including development of key campaigns and corporate messages, and overseeing curated content internal and external to the organisation. The team members' skills may include corporate or government communications, journalism, PR and digital marketing.

3. The Digital Implementation Team (website and social media)

This team is responsible for daily implementation: moderating and monitoring social media sites, pushing out messages based on the agreed campaign plan and engaging with their online community. The team will be made up of skilled digital marketing, social media marketing professionals, web and digital designers and website developers.

4. The Analytics Hub

Within this department the team is analysing the social intelligence garnered from monitoring and analytical tools and assessing the performance of proactive campaigns, in order to measure public sentiment in relation to the agency on different issues. The team will be highly skilled in digital analytics and social intelligence gathering and reporting and will have a background in digital marketing or data analysis.

5. Cloud Control

Within this department, the team manages the information technology (IT) infrastructure to support the entire 'Newsroom', from website hosting and security to reviewing and managing access to third-party cloud accounts and the data stored on each. IT and web management skills are required here.

Social media has an intrinsic role in emergency response management. But the challenge now is ensuring that policing, fire, ambulance, municipal authorities and other first-response organisations can swiftly integrate well-thought-out and developed social media strategies, effective monitoring systems and emotive campaigns that harness the power of the online community in a way that allows them to effectively carry out their duties. How does your emergency response agency plan to embrace an increasingly sophisticated Internet? You also need to accurately measure the return on investment of your social media activity in terms of:

- Resources, including capital, human and financial.
- Saving lives.
- Introducing efficiencies in public engagement and digital communications.

⊛ ⊛ ⊛ ⊛ ⊛

STRATEGIC SOCIAL MEDIA USE integrating monitoring technologies must now be part of the vision for all first responders. Ramping up social media beyond community engagement and PR purposes, with more focus on monitoring systems and saving lives, has to be a stated priority.

10

Hosting Events in a Hybrid World

In person and online, the need to create innovative event experiences

'You are on mute' reminds many of their introduction to video platforms such as Zoom. This author was using Zoom for many years before the pandemic, but its use, along with many other virtual meeting and video chat platforms, is now considered a fundamental way in which we communicate.

Events are a very typical tool in the public sector marketing pro toolbox, but how events are hosted has also been transformed in a post-pandemic world. Hybrid is the new normal as in-person events return, but the appetite for a virtual choice remains.

So how you re-write your event management checklist and strategy is key here, and having hosted in-person, wholly online and hybrid events for my own business and for clients, I am presenting the best checklist you will find out there.

If there's one thing we are reminded of as a result of the pandemic it is that human connection is vital in every aspect of our lives. Pre-COVID-19, the Public Sector Digital Marketing Summit was in person and lots of fun. Public sector pros from across Ireland came along and really enjoyed the time out of the office to focus on digital marketing for their agency. The networking was always a hit, as was getting a chance to get off the work Ferris wheel and open your mind to new digital tactics, ideas and trends.

There are many pros of in-person events, such as

- Human connection
- The emotional lift from being at an event with like-minded people
- Improved attention because of 'leaving work' physically
- A real intention to give the event your attention
- Atmosphere and experiential benefits

Our pandemic pivot

The Public Sector Digital Marketing Summit was cancelled in 2020 and I believe that was the right decision, despite speakers and a venue being provisionally booked. There was way too much uncertainty in March 2020 and our event was scheduled for mid-June.

Fast-forward a year and I wanted to bring it back; we usually need 10–12 weeks to bring it together, so I decided to move it wholly online for 2021. A date was chosen and the waitlist was opened.

The June date was moved to September and the work started on understanding how our signature summit would look like as a virtual conference. The theme of the event was easy for us. There was definitely an appetite to know how public sector marketing pros transformed their communications during the pandemic. So, the title from the outset was 'Public Sector Digital Marketing Summit 2021: Communications Lessons from COVID-19.'

Here's what we had to research and make decisions on (and fast).

- **The tech:** How would we livestream and on what platform?

- **The event app:** How would we ensure that all attendees, speakers and sponsors would be engaged and had an opportunity to participate in real time?

- **The attendee experience:** Ensuring that the reputation of our summit would not be negatively impacted or the brand devalued because of taking it online—how would we master this?

- **Marketing messaging:** How to communicate that the event, albeit online, was still worth taking the time to attend?

- **Added value:** What extra value could we add to the attendee experience and/or ticket?

- **Agenda:** What will the agenda look like?

- **Speakers:** Who will speak? Is this an opportunity to get global speakers who were perhaps out of our reach when the event was in person?

- **Timing and duration:** How long should each day be and should we host it one or two days?

7 Wins and 5 Lessons from the Virtual Summit

THERE ARE NO FAILURES when you take action in your marketing. There are lessons! I love a good life and business lesson because it's where the growth opportunity sits.

Wins

1. Whova event app proved hugely successful to manage the online event

2. Attracting global speakers with a different perspective from the Irish experience

3. Attendee engagement was off the digital Richter scale (see our metrics to follow)

4. Speaker access was a big win for attendees as speakers hung around to answer questions, engaged in conversation and listened to the other keynotes

5. The three-month on-demand access to the event app and replay videos for attendees were great added value

6. Content repurposing is easier from a virtual event

7. It still looked highly professional with our dedicated studio and branded speaker frames and live photography and videography throughout the two days for social coverage

Lessons

1. One day is enough for a virtual event; our event spanned two days

2. The date in mid-September was too early as August is a month for extended annual leave in public sector so it left our lead-in time tight (even though we had been planning for three months)

3. There is a general feeling that committing to an online conference won't work as you won't give it your full attention, so this format simply just doesn't suit some people

4. There will always be an element of attention-attack as attendees decided to dual screen and dual work, so not actually taking the time off from work to attend

5. There is not *less* work with a virtual event, there is new work and different work; there is more pressure to make it engaging and look and feel impressive online

2021 SUMMIT SUCCESS

Communications Lessons from COVID-19

HASHTAG REACH

975
total Tweets

24 text Tweets

18 replies

413 reTweets

525 links and images

91.3
sentiment score

neutral

positive

negative

6.3M
potential impacts

650K
potential reach

136
total
contributors

7
Tweets
per contributor

4.7K
followers
per contributor

Thoughts on hybrid events

Given all of this, event formatting takes lots of thought, and I think there is a lot to be said for hybrid events. I do believe that virtual has a place in the post-COVID-19 world, but we need to be mindful that this does not suit everyone. The need for human connection and the emotional intelligence insights that come with in-person meetings are still vital. So, with great customer experience, we need to serve our audiences based on what they need and want, and not what we want to deliver. I'm really happy I took the decision to host the summit virtually in 2021. I am a firm believer that everything you read or learn is academic until you take action. I had to do this for myself and learn the lessons by taking the journey.

2022 and beyond for event hosts and marketers

So, what's planned for 2022? Based on hosting in-person and virtual summits I've made the following decisions already! The live experience combined with the attendee feedback has helped me make these decisions about our next summit.

- It will be a one-day event
- It's going to be hybrid
- We will have an Irish venue
- We will also have a livestream for virtual attendees
- We will reuse our event app for all attendees
- We will continue to attract global speakers

2021 SUMMIT SUCCESS

Communications Lessons from COVID-19

THE CONTENT

8 keynotes

4 case studies

1 interview

3
panel
discussions

6
social media
workshops

6
digital marketing
workshops

THE PEOPLE

› **150** attendees
› **34** speakers
› **9** team members

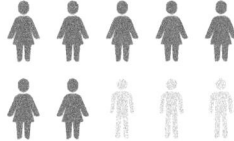

72%
of speakers
were female

TOPICS

› **Influencer Marketing**
› **Social & Live Video**
› **Email Marketing**
› **Content Marketing**

› **Hosting Virtual Events**
› **Podcasting**
› **Digital Crisis PR**
› **Digital Transformation Strategy**

11

How to Measure Success in Digital Communications

Understanding metrics that matter to public sector marketing pros

I often begin the development of a digital marketing strategy by measuring success. I want to know which metrics matter to the government or public sector agency that I am working with. Then I re-engineer my campaign and work backwards through my success framework.

Sprout Social defines social media metrics as 'data and statistics that give you insights into your social media marketing performance.' Some of these social metrics can be applied to all platforms—and methods of calculating the data—but some are specific to certain tools, and you need to learn those as well.

In this chapter I will show you how to measure engagement rates and other metrics, and how to use Google Analytics to your advantage.

Defining what you want from social media

In order to measure social media success, you need pre-defined goals. Social analytics will prove results, but you must ensure your goals are aligned with your organisation's vision and campaign objectives.

When measuring your goals against your objectives, consider the following:

- What is your organisation's tone of voice, and is your team and department agreed on how you will speak on social media?

- Do your social media goals align with your overall organisation or department goals?

- Is your team structure set up to deliver on those goals?

- What other investment is required to have a robust digital team, e.g., training, advertising budget, technology, equipment?

- What is your strategy for constant iteration and development, given the pace of digital change?

Setting SMART goals

The SMART framework can help you make sure your goals are agreed upon:

- **Specific:** Defining goals for a specific public interest need.
- **Measurable:** Understanding what metrics matter in your strategy or campaign.
- **Achievable:** Ensuring you have the resources to meet your targets.
- **Realistic:** Achievable within the constraints of staff time and budget.
- **Time sensitive:** A deadline or timeframe will focus minds and make your goals more achievable.

Some common and broad social media goals include:

- Increase brand awareness (campaign specific).
- Improve engagement rates with niche citizens on social networks.

- Increase online community across all social platforms.
- Increase onsite conversions by X% on specific landing pages.
- Increase social share of voice (on particular topics).
- Drive overall website traffic by X%.
- Increase referral traffic from X social network by X%.

Here is an example of how SMART goals might look in practice. The department of agriculture wants to increase engagement among their target audience (namely, farmers) over the next three months. Their SMART goals might be:

- **Specific:** Increase Facebook Page fan likes from farmers living in rural areas by 20%.

- **Measurable:** Increase link clicks on posts about the Common Agricultural Policy (CAP) by 15% and have an average post reach of 2,500 per post.

- **Achievable:** Yes, if we focus on creating video content for increased organic reach and engagement.

- **Realistic:** We will invest €500 in Facebook Ads.

- **Time sensitive:** The CAP campaign will run for three months.

Metrics that matter

So, when it comes to metrics, how do you analyse them, and how do you decide which metrics matter most? To begin, here are the two key types of social media metrics:

1. Vanity metrics

These are metrics that show you how many fans, followers or subscribers you have. But these are not necessarily the metrics that matter most on every platform or for every public sector or government agency.

2. Engagement rate

When you do the analysis from number of fans, followers, subscribers to engagement rate, the whole landscape changes. Now you are focused on how your content engages your citizens, as opposed to the total number of fans you have (knowing that many of them are probably not even seeing your content).

A framework for public sector digital communications measurement

To re-engineer your public sector campaigns for success, you can follow my measurement framework, which takes into consideration key performance indicators for public interest messaging. This framework has four key elements:

1. Percentage of audience engagement

Every campaign will identify the persona of the citizen you are targeting. In achieving true public engagement, you must set out a benchmark for success. What percentage of the population do you want to reach with your campaign?

EXAMPLE: *We want to target new mothers aged 20–29 whom we have identified as a key cohort in our vaccination programme.* By using the audience data in Facebook, you will be able to see how many women in this category you can potentially reach. You will mix this data with your own internal data sources and then build out your campaign.

2. Engagement barometer

To adequately evaluate the relevance of your content, you need to establish an engagement benchmark. See page 204 for benchmark metrics by platform, which you can use to compare your own results.

3. Conversion of social conversation to website engagement

Tracking social media engagement must follow on to tracking how much traffic your website has generated from your social media efforts. This data can be found in Google Analytics, but you can get richer data by adding your Facebook Page, Twitter, LinkedIn and Pinterest pixels to your website. (A pixel is a piece of tracking code that gives you more meaningful data. Each social network has instructions on where to find your account's pixel on their help sections.)

4. Social share of voice (sov)

It is important to understand how strong your voice is in big issues affecting the public and directly affecting your organisation. Social share of voice is a relatively new metric, coming directly as a result of big data. It helps you to understand how your public sector or government agency is performing in comparison to other voices on the social web around a particular topic or conversation.

There are many SaaS providers that can obtain this data for you, such as Talkwalker, Mention, Brandwatch or Brand24.

Understanding your metrics and measuring success

So, which specific metrics matter most for each platform, and what are the benchmarks? These are questions I get asked weekly. I recently wrote a report called *The State of Social Media in the Public Sector*, which was the very first primary study of social media use among 330 of Ireland's public sector agencies.

Central to this report was establishing which metrics I was going to analyse and how I measured successful social media activity against below-par performance. In deciding on the numbers, I wanted to use the opportunity to stress the importance of looking beyond vanity metrics.

The report reflected two key metrics:

1. Number of followers/fans/subscribers

2. Engagement rate (the collective number of engagement signals like, likes, comments, shares and clicks, divided by impressions)

Measurable engagement signals are different on different platforms. On Facebook, for example, it is how often a fan engages with your content. On Twitter, it is how much your followers are engaging with your Tweets. You can calculate your engagement rate on each platform by dividing the daily number of engagement signals (like, comment, share, reTweet, quote Tweet) by the number of fans or followers.

Social media benchmarks

So, what is a good engagement rate? Here are a few industry benchmarks:

Facebook
- \> 1% is good.
- 0.5%–0.99% is average.
- < 0.5% needs more work to define audience needs.

Twitter
- Between 0.09% and 0.33% is high, and you would expect to achieve 9–33 reactions for every 1,000 followers.

- Between 0.33% and 1% is very high, with expected reactions of 33–100 for every 1,000 followers.

Instagram
- The average rate is 3%.
- \> 3% and you are considered influential.

LinkedIn
- 2% is good.
- \> 2% is great.

YouTube
- Engagement on YouTube reflects how long your video is watched (also known as audience retention). You can find your audience retention report in YouTube Analytics.

- You can also count total viewer interactions, e.g., by adding likes, comments, favourites and shares together, and then dividing by the number of views. The higher the percentage, the better the engagement rate.

TikTok
- 5% is good.
- 10% is great.

Pinterest
- 11 rePins is average.
- 80% of all Pins are rePins.
- A Pin's lifespan is seven months.
- It takes a Pin 3.5 months to get 50% of its engagement.

Other important metrics your public sector or government agency should consider include:

- **Post interaction on Facebook:** This measures the fan engagement on posts by calculating the average amount of all interactions (likes, love, wow, haha, etc.), comments and shares per fan per post.

- **Tweet interaction:** The number of reactions divided by the number of Tweets on one day, then divided by the number of followers.

- **Instagram engagement:** This metric is calculated by dividing the interactions of users on one day by the number of followers. This includes comments and favourites.

Google Analytics for website measurement

Google Analytics showcases the power of digital marketing in a variety of ways. At your fingertips, you have data about your website visitors that you can use to target and improve your marketing efforts. In other words, the platform can be the guiding force behind the entirety of your marketing efforts.

Unfortunately, many organisations do not get to reap the rewards of Google Analytics. That is because, as powerful as the platform can be, it also has the potential for immense confusion. Log in for the first time, and the amount of metrics and charts staring at you may prompt you to log back out.

To get over that hump, and begin to take advantage of its power, here are terms, tips and tools that allow even marketing novices to make the most out of their Google Analytics account.

10 essential terms of Google Analytics

First, let's start with a quick vocabulary lesson. The following definitions help you make sense of the variety of metrics that Google Analytics can track and report on its default dashboards and in custom reports.

1. Sessions vs. users

The core metrics in many of your reports, and even your introductory dashboard, will be sessions and users. Sessions simply describe how many times someone had an experience on your website, meaning they entered at some point and left at another. Users, on the other hand, describe the amount of people who had those experiences.

2. Pageviews and unique pageviews

Total pageviews are somewhat self-explanatory. They differ from unique pageviews in that they count someone twice if they visit the same page twice. However, the same action only counts as one unique pageview.

3. New vs. returning visitors

How many of your website visitors arrive for the first time, or return from a past visit? This metric gives you a better idea of the answer, helping you determine how you should structure your content depending on your audience's existing level of familiarity.

4. Bounce and exit rate

Bounce rate counts the percentage of users who leave your website after seeing only a single page. For example, they may come to your homepage and leave without ever navigating deeper into your website. Exit rate, on the other hand, counts the users who leave from a certain page, even if they have visited other pages in the process.

5. Average time on site

How long your visitors stay on your website on average is an important metric to track. The more pages they visit, the longer they stay, and the higher their chances they will take the action you want them to take, or absorb the information you want them to absorb.

6. Traffic sources

In a variety of reports, you may come across this information. It describes where exactly your traffic comes from, either defined by you through a UTM code or based on knowledge Google can easily gather.

7. Search engine, direct and referral traffic

The three most common traffic sources will fall into one of these three categories. Search engine traffic can be broken down into paid (through Google Ads) and organic (unpaid). Direct traffic involves users directly typing your website URL into their browser, while referral traffic counts visits from users who clicked on a link on another website.

8. Source, medium and campaigns

Google Analytics allows you to track manually coded URLs to better evaluate your marketing efforts through its URL builder (available at ga-dev-tools.appspot.com/campaign-url-builder). You can pull each of these parameters into various reports, allowing you to track entire campaigns or individual tactics within these campaigns.

9. Goals and conversions

Google defines conversions more broadly than its competitors. You can set up goals like a minimum time spent on your website to a lead conversion, a specific sequence of pages visited and more. Then, you can evaluate your various traffic sources, demographics and more based on these goal conversions.

10. Goal value

You can set up an estimated value for each conversion. For example, you may attribute €500 for each citizen that signs up for a smoking cessation programme based on the cost to the health system of smoking-related illness.

5 tips to set up your Google Analytics dashboards

With the above terms in mind, it's time to take a closer look at the set-up of your dashboard. Here are five tips that can help you maximise the efficiency of the data provided through the platform.

1. Decide on whether you need custom

Google's standard dashboard focuses on a broad range of metrics that will be sufficient for many organisations. However, you can also go custom. There are many tutorials available online to help you build a custom dashboard that reports exactly what you are looking for.

2. Focus on your marketing goals

If you decide to build out a custom dashboard, make sure you eliminate all extraneous information. Take the opportunity to build out a platform specifically designed to help you accomplish your marketing and organisational growth goals.

3. Understand and leverage existing reports

Google Analytics allows you to report on website and visitor data based on your audience, traffic and conversions and user behaviour while on your site. The right dashboard offers a mix of two, helping you understand visitor demographics along with a better understanding of how those users act while visiting your website, and whether you are reaching your marketing goals.

4. Set up a variety of conversions

Customising your dashboard only makes sense if you know exactly what you want. Once you do, you can build a platform for yourself that includes a number of conversion goals specifically designed for your needs, from lead conversions to behavioural change.

5. Adjust as needed

Finally, don't treat your dashboard as a one-off project. Instead, take every opportunity you can to build and improve its features. If you find yourself not using some of the reports you have built, eliminate them in favour of more relevant metrics.

* * * * *

MEASUREMENT IS AS IMPORTANT as any other digital communication task you will complete. It is the window to the success or failure of your social media and digital marketing efforts. It also provides insights into how you need to improve, iterate or innovate your digital communications. Without measurement, you will never progress, and you will not understand how well your campaigns and ongoing corporate messaging are impacting the public.

Redefining Communications Roles and Work Practices in the Digital Age

How to introduce digital communications seamlessly into existing work plans

Our lives are changing and changing quickly, and so are the ways we communicate with each other. Google says that we are only 1% of the way into how technology is changing our lives, our workplaces and our businesses, which means that old ways of engaging with the public are becoming increasingly outdated. But is the public sector able to adapt, and, more importantly, is it willing to? That's the biggest challenge facing your organisation today.

During the early evolution of digital communications in government and public sector, IT or marketing teams were mainly responsible for launching a website or setting up a social media account. Today, digital communications should be an organisation-wide priority as every function has a role to play in digital storytelling, social media, content creation and curation, social customer service and online reputation management.

Many large public sector organisations have evolved their traditional marketing, press or communications departments into agency-like structures. Here is an infographic illustrating how this could work in practice with some sample departments:

DIGITAL TEAM

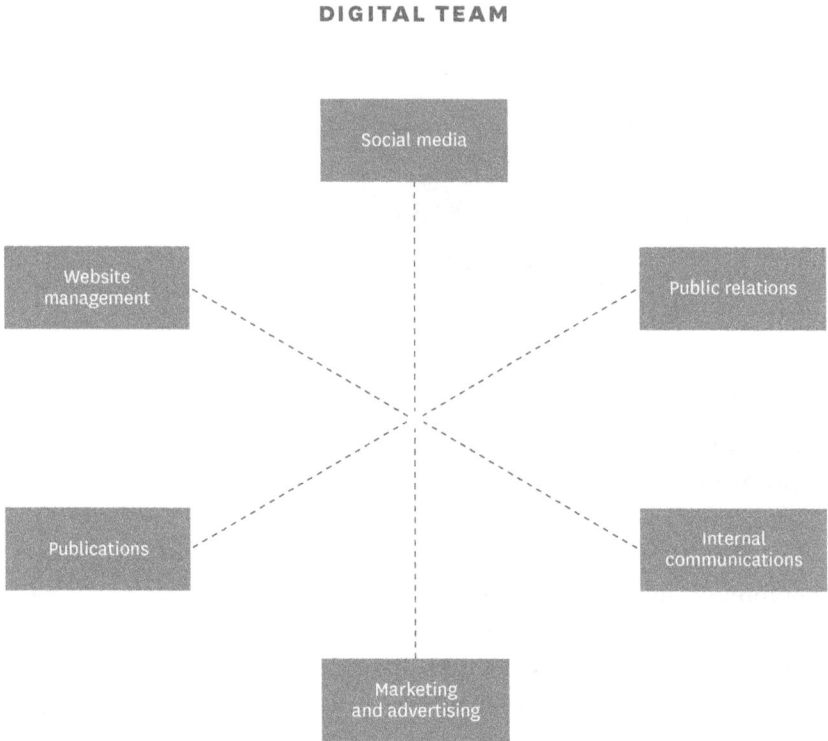

The responsibilities taken on by a newly formed or evolved digital team cannot survive the upward pressure and demands of organisation-wide digital communications needs. So how can you scale without creating a tipping point?

Total digital communications audit

To truly embrace digital communications in all its facets, you need to understand how digitally agile your organisation is. In chapter 4 I took you through all the steps to undertake an initial social media audit for each individual platform; here, I will show you how to take your organisation through a complete audit of your entire digital communications strategy.

A digital communications audit will capture what tasks you are currently undertaking in order to serve the entire organisation's needs. The audit needs to reflect the digital communications needs of each department to get a thorough understanding of how each needs to be served.

This audit should cover:

☐ **Full technical website audit and off-page SEO** to include all inbound links, site speed, mobile optimisation, re-directs, Google Business listing, Facebook Open Graph and Twitter Cards.

☐ **On-page SEO** to include focus keyword, internal and external links, tags, title, meta description, alt images, readability and sub-headings.

☐ **Google Analytics** to include 12-month review of traffic and performance to include goals and conversions, top 10 keywords driving most traffic, top 10 most viewed landing pages, Google organic traffic percentage of overall traffic, cross device conversions and top sources of traffic.

☐ **Social media digital footprint** to include number of accounts, user access and followers.

☐ **Social media** audit to include 12-month review of reach, engagement, community growth, content, community management, video views, video retention rate and branding. Turn to page 69 to see a full set of steps for a complete social media audit.

- [ ] **Social advertising** audit to include 12-month review of total spend, ROAS (return on ad spend), reach, engagement and top performing campaigns.

- [ ] **Email marketing** audit to include list number and percentage growth on previous 12 months, segmented databases, dormant users, compliance with regional privacy laws, campaign results, total number of campaigns, average open rate, average CTR (click-through rate), bounces and unsubscribes, source of subscribers and a review of your express permission policy.

- [ ] **Content marketing plan** to include personas for each audience segment, keyword research terms, content assets created, content performance per channel, content engagement rates and conversions.

- [ ] **Google PPC** to include total spend, ROAS, paid for traffic, CTR and conversion rate.

- [ ] **Influencers** identified with whom you can collaborate and who have an engaged audience that you want to target.

- [ ] **App review** to include app downloads, app engagement rates and app store optimisation.

- [ ] **Software as a service (SaaS)** audit to include all tools and software being used in the organisation, total spend, access rights, number of users, frequency of use and business case to renew or change supplier.

Identifying new signals for conversion

It is true that the fragmented customer journey is more difficult to measure in the Digital Age; however, there are rich signals being left by citizens with every digital touchpoint. Here are signals you can use to track your audience throughout all of your digital communications:

AUDIENCE SIGNALS AT EACH STAGE
OF THE CITIZEN JOURNEY

RESEARCH	ENGAGEMENT	CONVERSION
Google search	Download guide	Subscribe
Blog post	Share on social media	Sign-up
Social media	Landing page	Download checklist
Google search	Landing page	Subscribe
PPC ads	Web link click	Click to call
YouTube	Video view	Subscribe
Website search	Landing page	Complete form

Are you aware of the research, engagement and conversion stage of each citizen's journey that aligns with your campaign or organisational goals?

Key performance indicators

One of the biggest challenges for organisations in gaining true digital transformation from a communications perspective is the realisation that shared key performance indicators (KPIs) across all communications departments are necessary. Your transformation needs to include:

1. New job roles

There are jobs that exist now that didn't 10 years ago. However, I've witnessed a growing trend within public sector of simply 'giving' communications or interested staff a role to play in managing social media or taking on the new tasks in the absence of new hires. This can work if all or most of their existing workload is passed onto another staff member, but often social and digital are add-ons.

This creates fragmented and distracted delivery, and also what I describe as 'burden-bin' symptoms. Staff members who acquire digital communications tasks are dumped on with endless social media, content creation and web tasks without any strategic, creative or measurement framework. This approach will ultimately lead to box-checking broadcast social media, ad hoc online public engagement or worse errors online.

2. Job descriptions

Job descriptions are also outdated. When you decide to step out on your digital transformation path, staff may feel threatened, nervous and resistant, and display negativity towards change in work practices and taking on new digital communications tasks. In fact, some will cling to their existing (outdated) job descriptions as a way to prevent change from taking place.

A full audit of work practices needs to take place to ascertain:

- time spent on digital communications
- repeated tasks that could be automated
- number of staff involved in the citizen journey
- manual nature of tasks
- gaps in activity
- outdated systems
- misaligned priorities

3. New hires

Making a decision to hire new digital communications staff should be done in tandem with the restructuring of existing workflows.

4. Training

Ongoing continuing professional development is a must in today's world of digital disruption. Organisations that are having internal discussions about whether to embrace social media or not are already

light-years behind the curve. The changing algorithms, shifts in consumer behaviour, technology and mobile consumption dictate to
whom we should be responding and iterating our digital strategies.
While senior leadership should be directing the digital road map, the
influences are largely external.

5. Scaling digital skills

Introducing an internal Digital Skills Academy will help with true
digital transformation. Having a school of social and digital training
for staff which is built into their work plans will serve the organisation in the long-term. Departments should take responsibility for
their own social networks, contributing to blog and authority content
and being willing to go front of screen to engage with their audiences. All of this can be overseen by the head of digital (or equivalent
senior leader) and be included in the organisation's digital marketing
strategy. Standard operating procedures (SOPs) for specific digital tasks should be created, and if these are repeatable tasks, then
automation should be considered; for example, reviewing multiple
dashboards.

6. Automation

Speaking of automation, we live in a time where most manual tasks
can be automated and delivered more efficiently and effectively than
humans can do them. When you audit your team's work practices, a
list of all potentially automated functions can be created, from audience segmentation, social media management, content publishing
and social listening to crisis monitoring.

7. Technology

You need to budget for software to scale up and execute seamless
digital communications. Draw up a business case for each tool, and
complete price and feature comparisons.

8. Governance

Good governance is expected in public sector agencies. From a
digital transformation perspective, there will be new policies and

protocols required to reflect new work practices and activities. These include:

- social media use policy
- social media guidelines
- online brand guidelines
- tone of voice guidelines
- social network set-up protocol
- online abuse policy
- social customer service policy
- content curation guidance
- crisis communications protocol
- SOPs for individual digital communications tasks
- social media management tool access protocol
- social listening tool guidance
- online PR monitoring tool guidance

Facing the challenge of digital transformation

Being ready to face digital transformation means knowing how to take full advantage of practices already taking place. So if you're looking for inspiration, then where better to get it than from some of your peers who are leading the way? I asked six public sector marketing pros to share their experiences of transforming their communications in the S3 Age.

1. Social media as an effective recruitment tool

Aidan McGrath, former head of recruitment, Beaumont Hospital, Dublin
'As public service leaders, it's our responsibility to ensure our public services are staffed with the highest quality candidates. A recent study by Jobvite stated that, according to recruiters, the top investments for growing an employer brand are: social media (47%), company career website (21%) and marketing and advertising (12%). With this in mind, it is imperative that public service organisations

like Beaumont Hospital, whether large or small, harness and engage social media as part of their hiring process.'

2. The empowered citizen driving digital communications in the public sector

Cliona Connolly, Irish press officer, EPP Group, EU Parliament, Brussels
'The public sector has a responsibility to inform the public, whether that's as a legal obligation or as a moral duty to its citizens. Social media provides an array of innovative tools that reach a diverse range of people who may not otherwise hear or see our messages in traditional media. Then understanding your goals, identifying any interesting or valuable information you have and being creative in how you deliver it is key. You should also ensure you put the "social" in social media by engaging in two-way conversations, so you can build trust and create a loyal following. In short, you should always provide added value for your followers.'

3. Making your website the central hub for all communications

Laura Ryan, former head of marketing and communications, Limerick City and County Council
'Limerick.ie is a leader in digital communications for local government in Ireland. Why? Because it has been designed around its users in the community. Each user has their own private login, where they can create an individualised profile of interests, build itineraries on what to see and do in Limerick and see all their dealings with the Council. The aim of the site is to always present Limerick in a positive light, to give information about Limerick City and County Council services and be number one in searches for information on Limerick. We publish relevant and up-to-date content by working with partners in the region and in showcasing Limerick's unique selling points by providing information on visiting, investing, learning, living and events in Limerick. We're now setting the foundation for what people can do with the platform and what it can do for them. And we're developing these personalised services in an integrated way, so we can develop this experience for years to come.'

4. The university enhancing education with digital communications

Glenn Hurst, lecturer and associate professor, Department of Chemistry, University of York

'Advances in digital communications are transforming the way in which students are able to learn at all levels of study. Social media platforms such as Facebook, Instagram, Snapchat, Twitter and You-Tube have been utilised as a vehicle to significantly enhance the communication skills of learners together by providing a space to form an online community. Further to being able to utilise social media to enhance engagement of learners with subject matter, social media is also an effective tool for instructors to be able to provide additional feedback to students in a quick and easy manner. In short, use of social media as a learning aid is here to stay and we have embraced it at University of York.'

5. Leveraging the public for improved first response

David Bailey, former social media project lead, NPCC Digital Policing Portfolio, and former senior communications manager, Staffordshire Police

'Social media has massively aided policing. The public now expect to be able to ask the police a question and get an answer, and trust that answer. And they want to be able to have those conversations with us on the channels that they want to choose. Facebook means we can drive conversations locally to help us find missing people, identify offenders or educate around when you might need to take action or stay safe. Twitter works really well in getting updates or alerts out fast.'

6. Improving public safety through integrated communications

Jane Ryder, communications manager, Food Safety Authority of Ireland

'Having a presence on Twitter, Facebook and LinkedIn is essential for us as the food regulator. It enables us to reach a wider audience, to be proactive, to improve our customer service, to create awareness about our food industry events, to build a greater online profile, to build a community around food safety, to generate traffic to our website and to interact directly with our stakeholders. It's also proven essential if there's an issue with a food where the FSAI needs to get key messages out there quickly to consumers and the food industry. Social media is integrated into our communications strategy and is at the heart of our engagement with our stakeholders.'

* * * * *

THESE ARE JUST SIX of your peers who are implementing game-changing digital media strategies every day for their organisations. Isn't time you got on board, too?

Are you inspired to digitally transform your public sector communications? Stepping out on the road to digital transformation can be daunting, but it is also exciting to see just what can be achieved with the digital channels available to you.

Digital Maturity in the Engagement Age

Standing still is stagnation, evolution is relevance, scaling is making impact

During my time preaching the revolution of PR, media and marketing for government and public sector, my message has often fallen on deaf ears. I have felt like the high priestess of digital, preaching from the pulpit in meeting rooms, trying to rouse the organisation's disciples into leading the digital charge.

There are still many influential people in government and the public sector who believe that a digital-first approach is not needed, that social media is a bubble where the opposing public hang out and that e-commerce is slang for pyramid schemes. Don't get me wrong, I am all too aware of echo chambers, multi-level marketing and trolls, but when the boardroom fails to embrace the technological revolution, they are signing their own digital death warrant. Furthermore, when they commit digital communications to the remit of traditional press and marketing teams, they are strangling the organisation of opportunity and impact.

Digital transformation and scalability of implementation starts at the top and its progress is helped or hampered in equal measure by CEOs and senior decision makers. Organisations that discount digital transformation and organisation-wide scalability do so at their peril. In my experience, the digital dilemmas paralysing public sector boardrooms are the very same dilemmas inspiring agile private sector enterprises. Government organisations are finding it more difficult to reform, with many leaders not fully understanding the value of digital transformation, and so feeling ill-equipped to trigger the reform button. But smaller, more agile public sector bodies are braver and bolder, with an acute awareness that survival of the fittest means those that can adapt quickest.

Having an expansion mindset for constant transformation

Google (search) and Meta (social) are the goliaths of the Internet with TikTok leading the charge on their transformative social storytelling app. They are the controlling agents of digital communications, and failing to understand their role will quickly put you in an underdog position. By 10 a.m. there are one billion searches on Google, while one in every five minutes on the Internet is spent on social media. When people search, they are displaying an intent to be educated, entertained, sold to or convinced.

Users of social are seeking like-minded people to whom they can relate or aspire. The world of digital communications has storytelling as its central cog, with search and social using their shoulders to turn the wheels. Communities and niche influencers are stepping into voids that government and public sector fail to be relevant in and sources of news are now not always from newsmakers and mainstream media but Internet personalities.

I know that the world of the social web is a noisy place to navigate. I know there is a lot of white noise and notional influence, and worrying levels of misinformation there. I know prolonged hours swiping up, down, left and right is bad for your mental well-being. However,

I am inclined to step onto the side of digital opportunity and say that we can engage with stakeholders who can bring our organisation to the next level, who have the knowledge to fill a gap in our work or find an event that can put us in front of hundreds of citizens. Seven years ago I found myself delivering the keynote at the SMILE (Social Media, the Internet and Law Enforcement) conference to 150 chiefs of police from across the US and Canada in Phoenix, Arizona—all sparked by a Twitter conversation about my first book (*Social Media Under Investigation: Law Enforcement and the Social Web*).

Do not be a disruptor for the wrong reasons

There are so many stats I could throw your way to try to convince you that the power is no longer in your hands but in those of the Digital Age citizen. The smartphone has revolutionised the way we communicate, shop, travel, and engage with family and friends. There is no going back. The next billion users of the Internet will not just be mobile-first, they will be mobile-only—so the smartphone's significance will continue to grow. Your competition is not your competitor a few streets over, it is the best mobile experience being provided to your customer by companies such as Amazon and Netflix.

Step into the citizens' shoes, and be in their moments

But what is disruption in digital communications? Quite simply, it is closing the circle on your customer dialogue. The smartphone has changed the world, but more than that it has changed human behaviour. We look at it 200 times a day in 74-second bursts, seeking answers to our biggest and smallest problems.

Organisations need to ask themselves: *'Are we there to answer and to engage the public?'*

Digital transformation from a communications perspective is simply about having a 360-degree conversation with your citizens, stakeholders, colleagues or whomever the target audience may be. The age of the Internet has given everyone a voice, but it has turned the tables of power. Seated now at the top of the table are prosumers, active consumers with a newfound voice ready to use at any opportunity. The customer experience is the cog in the wheel of digital transformation. Social media has created engagement-ready citizens seeking real-time relationships with government and public sector organisations that impact their lives. Sitting sideways on the same seat are those goliaths of the Internet. So, if you want to take your seat at this digital dinner table, then you better sing for your supper.

Fail to disrupt, prepare to be disrupted: 10 tips to prepare for digital transformation

Give your organisation a sporting chance with digital transformation. Here are my top 10 tips to prepare for the biggest revolution in the modern age:

1. **You, not me.** Remember who's at the top table: your public, your citizen. They expect you to serve up exactly what they want, when and where they need it.

2. **Mobile gives you digital mobility.** The smartphone-in-my-pocket (or handbag) lifestyle has reformed personal behaviour, including consumption of content and the speed of decision-making.

3. **Agility is a head start.** If you've been training in the digital gym and flexing your transformation muscles, then you're ready to make the changes. Agility is a key ingredient to impactful reform.

4. **Trust is currency in the post-pandemic age.** Those who have earned the public's trust are controlling the Internet. The fake news explosion happened because those engaged in it had a shrewd knowledge of how to rank, optimise and target. It is time you caught up.

5. **Small changes amass big wins.** Implementing best practice across all digital channels pays off. A simple open-graph implementation

on your website will ignite new traffic sources, while the use of social pixel tracking will help you build custom audiences. Small is big in the Digital Age.

6. **Social storytelling, please.** Our brains are wired to remember stories more than 22 times better than just facts and figures alone. Use stories to trigger conversations that lead to engagement and conversions. Tell your 'once upon a time' story.

7. **Open the parachute and jump.** Don't wait for perfection, you have to jump in to see what needs to be improved. Taking action will pay off. Experience is the best teacher.

8. **Be different, be you.** The brand or voice you have built up to now needs to be amplified with digital communications tactics. But keep the personalisation and that differentiation, because in an age where the Internet continues to expand, uniqueness and resonance will pay off.

9. **Transform with purpose.** Transform because of your 'why', not because you feel pressured. The purpose of your digital journey— ultimately, to benefit your citizen—will keep you focused and motivated.

10. **Stick with it.** Change is constant, digital change is rapid. This is not a sudden re-direction we are taking; we are on a new road. Please take the path to transformation.

Ready, steady, scale

So are you ready, willing and able to evolve and scale digital communications in your organisation? If you don't change your mindset, the decision will be out of your hands. Let me give you some friendly advice: don't worry about the 'how' right now. Your role as CEO, director or manager or public sector marketing pro is to position digital front and centre in the culture, in the attitudes of the boardroom and then on the frontlines. I promise that you will figure out the how-to along the way. Knowledge requires action and skills need practice. Learn from what doesn't work and allow me to be your digital mentor and muse.

Stop scrolling and start taking action. Empower your people to be leaders and lightworkers online. Democracy, science and public trust are all at risk. If you fail to act, then you are part of the problem. If you are inspired to act, then you can become part of the collective action that takes on debilitating cyber-warfare in the form of fake news and misinformation. There is nobody else to take your place online. As the trusted source, subject matter expert, legitimate proponent of public policy specific to your area, it is both your role and responsibility. If you do not lead online, you are making space—and, I would argue, inviting bad actors determined to subvert the truth to fill that space, thereby contributing to the infodemic. The pandemic has shown how trust rises to the top over misinformation—it is not time to rest; it is time to rise up online and scale digital communications within your department and organisation. This is one of the most valuable lessons learned from living through a pandemic.

Endnotes

Introduction

p. 2   *video messaging on Facebook increased by 70% just one month after the world was plunged into a pandemic*: Katie Collins, 'Facebook Sees 70% Increase in Messenger Group Video Calls following Coronavirus Outbreak', CNET; available at https://www.cnet.com/tech/services-and-software/facebook-sees-surge-of-engagement-worldwide-following-coronavirus-outbreak/

Chapter 1

p. 10   *why citizens are accessing news on social and who they are interested in listening to and learning from*: Nic Newman et al., 'Reuters Institute Digital News Report 2021: 10th Edition', Reuters Institute and University of Oxford; available at https://reutersinstitute.politics.ox.ac.uk/sites/default/files/2021-06/Digital_News_Report_2021_FINAL.pdf

Chapter 2

p. 24   *there were 4.9* billion *Internet users in the world by December 2021*: 'Number of Internet Users Worldwide from 2005 to 2021', Statista; available at https://www.statista.com/statistics/273018/number-of-internet-users-worldwide/

p. 24   *number of mobile phone users worldwide today surpasses six billion*: 'Number of Smartphone Subscriptions Worldwide from 2016 to 2027', Statista; available at https://www.statista.com/statistics/330695/number-of-smartphone-users-worldwide/

p. 25   *reviews by consumers have become perhaps the single biggest influencer of buying decisions*: 'New Study Highlights the Importance of Online Reviews in Local Search,' Social Media Today; available at https://www.socialmediatoday.com/marketing/new-study-highlights-importance-online-reviews-local-search

p. 26   *On Facebook, for example, we have on average about 338 friends*: 'What People Like and Dislike about Facebook', Pew Research; available at http://www.pewresearch.org/fact-tank/2014/02/03/what-people-like-dislike-about-facebook

p. 28   *social media use increased and it became an important enabler in human connection during multiple lockdowns*: Colleen McClain et al., 'The Internet and the Pandemic', Pew Research Center; available at https://www.pewresearch.org/internet/2021/09/01/the-internet-and-the-pandemic/

p. 30   *90% of the information we process is visual*: Visual Teaching Alliance, http://visualteachingalliance.com

p. 30   *more than 80% of the entire Internet would consist of video*: '2017: The Year of Visual Content', Digital Marketing Institute; available at https://digitalmarketinginstitute.com/en-us/blog/2017-7-18-2017-the-year-of-visual-content

p. 30   *transforming their social media presence specifically to account for this trend*: 'Social Media Has Transformed Consumer Expectations', Curalate; available at https://www.curalate.com/blog/social-media-consumer-expectations

p. 30   *when users express a question or concern to a brand on Twitter, they expect a response within an hour*: Ibid.

p. 30   *taking longer than five minutes to respond to a new lead will decrease customer conversion rates*: '5 Minutes or Less: Risk and Reward in Lead Response Time', Vendasta; available at https://www.vendasta.com/blog/lead-response-time

p. 31   *The TikTok explosion made it the number one downloaded app in 2021*: John Koetsier, 'Top 10 Most Downloaded Apps and Games of 2021: TikTok, Telegram Big Winners', *Forbes*; available at https://www.forbes.com/sites/johnkoetsier/2021/12/27/top-10-most-downloaded-apps-and-games-of-2021-tiktok-telegram-big-winners/?sh=3239f3da3a1f

Chapter 3

p. 46   *use search throughout the decision-making journey to get advice on purchases*: 'The Demanding Consumer: Expecting Tailored Experiences', Think with Google; available at https://www.thinkwithgoogle.com/consumer-insights/meetingconsumerexpectations

p. 47   *54% of adult Internet users regularly create and share photos and videos*: 'Photo and Video Sharing Grow Online', Pew Research Center; available at http://www.pewinternet.org/2013/10/28/photo-and-video-sharing-grow-online

p. 47   *Photos are also the most common form of UGC created by millennials*: 'How to Use User-Generated Content Marketing to Reach and Convert Millennials', Trustpilot; available at https://business.trustpilot.com/reviews/how-to-use-user-generated-content-marketing-to-reach-and-convert-millennials

p. 47   *Product reviews make up 29% of UGC*: Ibid.

p. 47   *The 25–34 (millennial) age group watches the most online videos*: '37 Staggering Video Marketing Statistics for 2018', Wordstream; available at https://www.wordstream.com/blog/ws/2017/03/08/video-marketing-statistics

Chapter 4

p. 64   *In 10 years, to 2021, there has been a 217% increase in social media use*: Simon
Kemp, 'Digital 2022: Global Overview Report', DataReportal; available at
https://datareportal.com/reports/digital-2022-global-overview-report

p. 82   *If you have fewer than 10,000 followers, you should post one or fewer times
per day*: 'How Often Should You Post on Facebook?', HubSpot; available at
https://blog.hubspot.com/marketing/facebook-post-frequency-benchmarks

p. 82   *The 55 top-performing brands on Instagram post, on average, 1.5 times per day*:
'Engagement Behaviour on Instagram', Unionmetrics; available at https://
unionmetrics.com/resources/brands-on-instagram

p. 82   *brands that Tweeted 2–5 times per day had the highest response rate*: 'Find Out
the Ideal Tweet Frequency for Brands', Socialbakers; available at https://
www.socialbakers.com/blog/1847-tweeting-too-much-find-out-the-ideal-
tweet-frequency-for-brands

p. 83   *you'll reach at least 60% of your audience*: LinkedIn for Small Business,
https://business.linkedin.com/grow

p. 83   *it is best to pin 3 or more times per day on Pinterest*: 'The Best Time to
Post on Instagram, Facebook, Twitter, LinkedIn, Pinterest, and Google+',
HubSpot; available at https://blog.hubspot.com/marketing/best-times-
post-pin-tweet-social-media-infographic

Chapter 5

p. 101   *average word-count on a piece of content that ranks on the first page of Google's
search engine results pages*: 'Ideal SEO Content Length', Sweor; available at
https://www.sweor.com/seocontentlength

p. 108   *list of the graphic dimension requirements for each social network*: 'Always
Up-to-Date Guide to Social Media Image Sizes', Sprout Social; available at
https://sproutsocial.com/insights/social-media-image-sizes-guide

Chapter 6

p. 111   *stories are up to 22 times more memorable than facts and figures*: 'Harnessing the
Power of Stories', Stanford University; available at https://womensleadership.
stanford.edu/stories

p. 111   *Stories are commanding record consumption rates*: '62 Must-Know Live Video
Streaming Statistics', Livestream.com; available at https://livestream.com/
blog/62-must-know-stats-live-video-streaming

p. 111   *Audiences are drawn to the story behind the story*: Ibid.

p. 119   *In 2021, 82% of the content on the Internet was video*: 'VNI Global Fixed and
Mobile Internet Traffic Forecasts 2017–2022', Cisco; available at https://
www.cisco.com/c/en/us/solutions/service-provider/visual-networking-
index-vni/index.html

Chapter 7

p. 122 *the majority of online traffic coming from video*: 'VNI Global Fixed and Mobile Internet Traffic Forecasts 2017–2022', Cisco; available at https://www.cisco.com/c/en/us/solutions/service-provider/visual-networking-index-vni/index.html

p. 122 *82% of all global Internet traffic will come from video views and downloads*: '135 Video Marketing Statistics You Can't Ignore in 2022', InVideo; available at https://invideo.io/blog/video-marketing-statistics/

p. 122 *Social media users are watching 100 minutes of video per day*: Ibid.

p. 132 *85% of people view videos with the sound off on Facebook*: '85 Percent of Facebook Video Is Watched without Sound', Digiday UK; available at https://digiday.com/media/silent-world-facebook-video

p. 137 *Video searches using the words 'how to' grew 70%*: 'I Want-to-Do Moments: From Home to Beauty', Think with Google; available at https://www.think withgoogle.com/marketing-resources/micro-moments/i-want-to-do-micro-moments

Chapter 8

p. 146 *the biggest challenges facing public sector around CX are four-fold*: 'The Public Sector Gets Serious about Customer Experience', McKinsey; available at https://www.mckinsey.com/industries/public-and-social-sector/our-insights/the-public-sector-gets-serious-about-customer-experience

p. 147 *there are five key trends driving satisfaction in 2022*: 'CX Trends 2022: Unlock Growth with Customer Service', Zendesk; available at https://www.zendesk.com/customer-experience-trends/

Chapter 9

p. 180 *Of the 4.5 billion social media users, 99% access their accounts via their mobile phone*: 'Social Network Usage & Growth Statistics', Backlinko; available at https://backlinko.com/social-media-users

Chapter 11

p. 199 *Sprout Social defines social media metrics as*: 'All of the Social Media Metrics That Matter', Sprout Social; available at https://sproutsocial.com/insights/social-media-metrics-that-matter

Chapter 12

p. 218 *according to recruiters, the top investments for growing an employer brand are*: '2018 Recruiter Nation Survey', Jobvite; available at https://www.jobvite.com/jobvite-news-and-reports/2018-recruiter-nation-report-tipping-point-and-the-next-chapter-in-recruiting

Conclusion

p. 224 *one in every five minutes on the Internet is spent on social media*: '1 Out of Every 5 Minutes Is Spent on Social Networking', LotLinx; available at https://www.lotlinx.com/vintenders-blog/1-every-5-minutes-spent-social-networking-facebook-still-1-digital-audience-penetration-engagement/

p. 225 *We look at it 200 times a day in 74-second bursts*: 'Here's How Many Times We Touch Our Phones Every Day', *Business Insider*; available at http://uk.businessinsider.com/dscout-research-people-touch-cell-phones-2617-times-a-day-2016-7

Glossary

Algorithm: A set of steps for completing a process or solving a problem. Social media algorithms are a set of technical elements and rules that control the content visible to users. They are constantly being updated. Algorithms are written and managed by software engineers, data scientists, content strategists and other experts to control what we see in our social newsfeeds and search engines.

Analytics: Digital marketing analytics measure metrics like traffic, leads and conversions, and allow marketers to observe which online events determine the actions users are taking at various digital touchpoints along the customer journey.

Annotations: YouTube annotations are additions, like text and links, that you can layer over your videos on your channel. These annotations let the viewer go further into the subject, providing a more interactive viewing experience.

App: Apps (short for 'applications') are programmes that you can download onto your mobile device and that are accessible through an icon on your home screen.

App store optimisation (ASO): Similar to search engine optimisation (SEO), ASO is the process of improving an app's metadata so that it ranks more highly on app stores like Google Play or Apple's App Store, and can be more easily found by potential users.

Artificial intelligence (AI): Also known as machine intelligence, AI is a discipline of computer science that seeks to train machines and systems to act and react independently, like humans.

Audience segmentation: This process involves categorising your audiences so that you can tailor messages and advertising to match their needs.

Audiogram: An audio file that combines images and captioned text overlays to create a video for sharing on social media.

Augmented reality (AR): AR uses immersive video and audio technology to overlay virtual objects and experiences onto the real world.

Automated marketing: The process of using software and technology to automate repeated marketing tasks for greater efficiency and effectiveness.

Backlink: An incoming link from one website to another. Having more backlinks, and backlinks from sites with good domain authority, improves your own website's authority with Google, resulting in higher rankings on search engine results pages (SERPs).

Big data: This is publicly available data, gathered from the Internet and social media, that can be used to create actionable insights. Digital marketers use big data to create highly targeted advertising campaigns.

Blogging: Writing a series of conversational articles that are posted online in chronological order. Blogs are typically hosted on a website, and are searchable by topic using tags.

Bounce rate: Your bounce rate is the share of your online visitors who leave your site after only looking at one page.

Call to action (CTA): The use of words or phrases to direct social media or website visitors to take a prompt and specific action.

Chatbot: Used in Facebook and website marketing, a chatbot uses artificial intelligence to conduct human-like conversations using audio or text.

Citizen journey: This is a road map or journey that your audience takes through their online experience. Using this map, you can share tailored messages on relevant social networks and your website.

Click-through rate (CTR): The ratio of people who click on a link to your website landing page to the number of total users who viewed that link on an ad, on social media or in an email.

Community management: The act of taking charge of your social media community from conversation to conversion.

Content marketing: Using content in multiple formats to engage social media users and website visitors.

Content marketing funnel: The process of moving your citizens from awareness to engagement, consideration and conversion.

Conversion marketing: The act of compelling a website visitor or social media fan to take a defined action, like a purchase or a sign-up.

Cost per click (CPC): Cost per click refers to the actual price you are being charged for each click in Google or other social media advertising campaigns in which the advertiser pays per click.

Cost per lead (CPL): A pricing model in which an online advertiser pays outright for each sign-up from an interested consumer. The advertiser can then follow up with the individual to attempt to convert them into a customer.

Cost per thousand impressions (CPM): The cost to an advertiser for each set of 1,000 people they reach through a particular online advertising campaign.

Cross-device conversion: A method of tracking sales that happen when a customer clicks an ad and then completes the conversion on another device or platform—for example, clicking on a Google

Ad on their computer, then later finding the product on their mobile device through Google search and making a purchase.

Customer experience (CX): The sum total of citizens' perceptions and feelings resulting from interactions with you, often greatly influenced by your timely communication with them online, on the social channels of their choosing (Social CX).

Customer relationship management (CRM): A centralised marketing automation tool designed to convert site visitors to leads and customers with the help of bulk mail sending, automated mails and lead nurturing. CRM also hosts your customer data.

Dark posts: *See* unpublished posts.

Digital PR: The discipline of adding digital marketing tactics to traditional PR efforts.

Domain authority: The domain authority of a website describes its relevance for a specific subject area or industry. This relevance score, ranked from 1–100, has a direct impact on its ranking by search engines such as Google.

Echo chamber: A term used to describe how social media users often engage only with content that they already believe in. Echo chambers are said to amplify and reinforce these beliefs, shutting out other competing views or opinions.

Email marketing: The act of sending a targeted message to a group of people with shared interests through email. Think newsletters or e-zines.

Embedding: Embedding refers to the integration of links, images, videos, gifs and other content into social media posts, blogs or website landing pages. Using embedded content can increase click-through rates, content engagement and conversion rates.

Engagement: When a person takes an action on your social media or website content, such as a like, share, comment, reTweet or click, it is considered engagement.

Engagement rate: This is a highly valuable social media marketing metric that measures the level of interaction that a piece of content is receiving from its audience.

Episodic series: A linked series of videos, podcasts, blog posts or livestreams that are released as individual episodes at regular intervals to encourage greater engagement and audience retention.

Evergreen content: Content is called evergreen when it is not time sensitive and will not go out of date quickly.

Exit page: This is the last page a user visits on your website before they leave or end their session.

E-zine: An email marketing newsletter.

Facebook Open Graph: Facebook's Open Graph API (application programming interface) allows you to customise your original Facebook content with a featured image, title and description so you can control how it appears when it's shared from your website.

Fake news: The deliberate sharing of misinformation online for individual or organisational gain. Fake news is an S3 Age form of propaganda.

Focus keyword: In search engine optimisation, this is the main keyword that you want to rank for in your search engine results, so that people who search for this keyword may find your blog post or landing page.

Frequent nasty comments (FNCs): My own framework for managing public conversations and digital PR crises on social media whereby you document all nasty and negative comments received and pre-prepare responses that are agreed upon by the organisation.

Funnel: In digital marketing, a funnel is a set of tactics and techniques you use to constantly direct new leads into your organisation in the hope that they convert. In planning models, this funnel is often presented as an upside-down pyramid.

Gamification: The use of traditional game-design tactics combined with technology to achieve greater engagement online.

GDPR: The General Data Protection Regulation is an EU privacy and data protection law that puts controls on how organisations can collect, store and use customer data.

Goals: In digital marketing, goals refer not to your own aims but to the defined actions you want your audience to take online.

Google Ads: Google's online advertising platform, which allows you to present a customised ad that appears in Google search results and across other online platforms when a user searches for a particular word or phrase.

Google Analytics: A free tool from Google to analyse your website traffic.

Google Search Console: Previously knowns as Google Webmaster, this is a no-charge web service

for website managers that allows you to check your indexing status and optimise the visibility of your website.

Hashtag: A word or phrase preceded by a hash or pound symbol (#) that allows people to find and post messages relating to a specific topic. These are particularly useful on Twitter, TikTok, Instagram and LinkedIn.

Impressions: In digital marketing, an impression is a view or an ad view, defined by somebody actually seeing your content. Impressions relate to CPM, which refers to cost per 1,000 impressions.

Inbound links: The same as a backlink, this is a link from another website to yours.

Inbound marketing: A digital marketing tactic designed to draw audiences in rather than push messages on them. An example would be blogging or search engine optimisation.

Influencer marketing: The tactic of partnering with an individual who has a significant online following because of a niche or shared interest. Influencer marketing is focused on social media in particular.

Infographic: A visual representation of data or statistics in a well-designed graphic.

InMail: A private message service in LinkedIn, allowing you to contact users you are not connected with. You have to have a Premium LinkedIn account to use InMail.

Keyword research: This is the practice of improving search engine optimisation by learning what alternate keywords or phrases your target individuals are using most.

Landing page: A single page on a website that features one clear message or call to action. Sometimes referred to as a sales page, lead capture page, static page, squeeze page or destination page, it is typically created as the entry point for users brought to your site from an advertising campaign or similar promotion. These pages are highly targeted, and typically have high conversion rates.

Lead magnet: An incentive that is offered in exchange for an individual's email address or other contact information. This often takes the form of downloadable digital content, such as e-books, how-to guides or PDF checklists, or the ability to access web videos or other multimedia.

Learning management system (LMS): A software application allowing you to deliver online education. It manages the administration, documentation, tracking, reporting and delivery of your courses.

Listicle: A blog post or an article that uses a list structure to share information. It is a highly engaging form of online content because of its ease of reading.

Livestream: A live broadcast on social media or through a website.

Long-tail keyword: A group of SEO-optimised words or phrases that target specific topics or niche audiences. For example, 'digital marketing for government agencies' is a long-tail keyword compared to simply 'digital marketing'. Long-tail keywords are more specific, and are often face less competition in keyword advertising.

Machine learning: A subset of artificial intelligence, this is the development of computer programmes that can learn from processing data.

Meta: Meta is the parent organisation of Facebook, Instagram, WhatsApp and Oculus.

Metaverse: A 3D version of the Internet where users (individuals and organisations), through VR, AR and other technologies, can interact with each other in the digital world.

Metric: A quantifiable measure of one specific piece of data in digital marketing.

Millennial (or Gen Y) marketing: These are specific digital marketing tactics that target those born between the early 1980s and the early 2000s.

Mobile optimisation: The process of ensuring that your visitors have a fully immersive and seamless experience when viewing your website on their smartphone.

Moderation: The act of controlling user-generated content, such as comments, that are posted on your website or on your social networks.

Native video: Video that is uploaded directly to any social network, as opposed to a video from a third-party site that is shared via a link.

News-jacking: The practice of adding your ideas or opinions to a breaking news story to generate free media coverage and social media engagement.

Off-page SEO: A set of techniques to improve the position of a website in search engine results pages (SERPs). An example would be getting more backlinks to your website.

Online reputation management: Influencing what the Internet says about you, your organisation or your brand.

On-page SEO: The practice of adjusting both the content and the source code of web pages to earn higher ranking in search engines to attract targeted visitors.

Optimisation: The practice of improving online content so that it is both discoverable and engaging. Optimisation can be used for search engine ranking, improving how graphics are displayed on specific social networks, improving the open rates of e-zines or improving how landing pages appear on smartphones.

Page speed: A measurement of how long it takes the content on your web page to load.

Pageviews: The number of views an individual web page has during a specific timeframe.

Payment gateway: The merchant service provided by an e-commerce provider to allow for credit card or direct payments such as PayPal, Stripe or Shopify.

Pay per click (PPC): PPC is an Internet advertising model in which an advertiser pays a publisher when their ad is clicked. PPC is most commonly associated with Google and other search engines.

Persona profile: A persona profile (or buyer persona) is a fictional representation of your ideal customer or audience. Persona profiles are used to help digital marketers better understand and target their audience, to better meet their needs.

Pixel: A piece of code that collects information about a visitor to your website and their behaviour on that site.

Podcast: Audio content produced in episodes and made available to stream live or download.

Reach: In website marketing, reach is the number of unique visitors your website sees per month. In social media marketing, reach is the number of people that have seen a piece of your content.

Reels: Short, vertical social media videos on Facebook and Instagram that can include multiple clips, filters, captions, interactive backgrounds, stickers and more. They are similar to TikTok videos.

Referral traffic: Found in Google Analytics, this is a measure of visitors who came to your website from multiple sources including social networks, email links or organic search.

Relevance score: A Facebook metric that rates the quality of your ad on its platform. The score given is between 1 and 10. The better the score, the lower the cost per click. In Google Ads, this score is called a Quality Score.

Repurpose: The practice of recycling your content for another social network or digital channel in order to reach more people.

Retargeting: A form of targeted advertising based on user's history of online activity, which is tracked using programmes called pixels and digital markers called cookies. This is also known as remarketing.

Return on ad spend (ROAS): A metric used to determine the results of an advertising campaign. Measuring and comparing ROAS can tell you which methods work best and help you make your campaigns more effective.

Search engine optimisation (SEO):
The practice of improving the relevance of your website and individual landing pages so that it can be found more easily by your target audience. SEO tactics include keyword research, backlinks, mobile optimisation, page speed and more.

Search engine results pages (SERPs):
This is the list of results a search engine like Google delivers when a user types in a search query.

Search marketing: A set of tactics to improve organic traffic to your website from search engines.

Sentiment: A metric to evaluate how people feel about your content or brand online. It is usually broken into three measures: positive, negative or neutral. Use of emoticons on social media can also signal sentiment, but there are many types of software available that use artificial intelligence and machine learning to capture this at scale.

Sessions: A metric used to define a group of interactions one user takes within a given timeframe on your website. Google Analytics defaults to 30 minutes, so whatever a user does on your website (e.g., browse pages, download resources, purchase products) within 30 minutes equals one session.

Share of voice (SOV): Specifically related to social media, this concept is used to refer to a brand or organisation's own advertising activity as a percentage of all ad activity across the whole sector or category type. It can also be used to monitor share of voice on topics of interest across the social web, including organic campaigning.

Smart glasses: Wearable computer glasses that offer wireless connectivity and other 'smart' features.

Social listening: The practice of monitoring what people are saying about you, individuals in your organisation, your brand or particular topics or keywords, for the purposes of writing content or preparing PR statements. This is done at scale by software that uses artificial intelligence and machine learning, generating more integrated results than manual Google searches or Google Alerts.

Software as a service (SaaS): A method of software delivery and licensing in which software is accessed online via a subscription, rather than bought and installed on individual computers.

Stories: Ephemeral (self-deleting) content that is a mix of photos, videos, text, animation and stickers created by social media users and shared on certain social networks (specifically Facebook, Instagram, TikTok and Snapchat). Stories are typically produced in vertical format (when you hold your phone in portrait style).

Swipe-up: The practice of clicking on a link on an Instagram Story by swiping up. To access this feature, click on the link icon when you create a Story and paste in the destination URL.

Talking head: A person talking to a camera screen, without the use of any background, stock or cutaway footage to break up the piece.

Targeted advertising: An online advertising campaign that is targeted at a particular group of people with shared demographic data, media interests or online behaviours.

Trust marketing: Creating content and messaging to improve trust in your organisation or in a public figure.

Twitter Cards: A service in Twitter that lets you and people who link to you attach photos, videos and other media experiences to Tweets in order to drive traffic to your website.

Unique pageviews: In Google Analytics, a unique pageview is the aggregate number of pageviews seen by a user during a single session.

Unpublished posts: Also referred to as dark posts, these are Facebook posts that are seen by only those specifically targeted in your Facebook advertising. Unpublished posts are set up and launched from Facebook Business Manager.

User experience (UX): UX deals with both usability as an integral part of the user experience, but also with a user's feelings, attitudes and behaviours when they interact with your product or service online. It is a function of web design.

User-generated content (UGC): Any content that is created by users, rather than by the creators or hosts of a website or social media platform. UGC can take the form of text, videos, photos, gifs, memes and so on. This type of content can be seen as a powerful form of support for your campaign, particularly when linked back to you with a link, hashtag (#) or mention (@).

User interface (UI): This is how a website or digital application looks, and how the user interacts with it.

UTM tracking: A UTM (urchin tracking module) is a piece of code in your website that lets Google Analytics see where searchers came from and what campaign or post led them to you.

Vanity metrics: Measures of online activity that are not necessarily actionable and may not accurately reflect important matters like active users, engagement, return on investment or revenue. Vanity metrics include number of users, number of downloads, raw pageviews and more.

Video retention rate: How long a viewer watches your video, usually calculated as a percentage of the total viewing time.

Virtual reality: Virtual reality (VR), or computer-simulated life, immerses users in a fully artificial digital environment.

Visual storytelling: The practice of engaging users in your content by using infographics, photos or videos to create emotion around that story.

Vlog: A video diary or video blog.

Webinar: An online meeting or workshop using third-party software that allows other people to engage with you through text chat or conversation.

Resources

THE RESOURCES IN this section are recommended because I use them in my own work. I have categorised them by digital marketing tactic.

Domain authority

- Website Authority Checker: Check the number of incoming links and referring domains to your website. https://smallseotools.com/domain-authority-checker
- Ahrefs Backlink Checker: Establish which prominent sites are backlinking to your site. https://ahrefs.com/backlink-checker

Page speed

- Google's PageSpeed Insights Tool: Check the speed load times of your website. https://pagespeed.web.dev

Keyword research

- Google Keyword Planner: A Google Ads tool to search for keywords and see how a list of keywords might perform in a PPC campaign. This tool is only available to those using Google's advertising platform. https://adwords.google.com/ko/keywordplanner
- Keywords Everywhere: A free Chrome or Firefox keyword research extension that generates hundreds of relevant long-tail keywords for any topic. The tool also shows you monthly search volume, cost-per-click and competition data of keywords on multiple websites and on YouTube. https://keywordsevery where.com

Content optimisation

- HubSpot's Blog Idea Generator: A free tool that will give you a year's worth of blog post ideas. https://www.hubspot.com/blog-topic-generator
- Blog Title Generator: SEOPressor's Blog Title Generator gives you catchy topic headlines and titles for book chapters, magazine or blog articles or Facebook or YouTube videos. https://seopressor.com/blog-title-generator
- Blog Post Headline Analyser: A free headline analyser tool from Co-Schedule that will score your overall headline quality and rate its engagement level. https://coschedule.com/headline-analyzer
- Social Message Optimiser: Another free tool from Co-Schedule that helps you optimise your social message by evaluating your copy, link and image or video. https://coschedule.com/social-message-optimizer

Graphics

- Canva: A free and paid for tool for non-graphic designers that offers layout and social media templates. https://www.canva.com
- Adobe Express: A paid tool with everything to create logos and graphics, flyers and posters, ads, banners and more with simple drag-and-drop functions and access to tons of Adobe fonts and images. https://www.adobe.com/express/learn/blog/introducing-creative-cloud-express

Audio and video

- Zoom: Cloud-based video conferencing software that has free and paid-for features and is accessible on desktop, tablet and phone. https://zoom.us
- Wavve: Software that turns audio highlights from your podcast, music or recordings into shareable social media videos. https://wavve.co
- Promo: High-quality template videos with access to a library of stock footage and royalty-free music for engaging audiences online. https://promo.com
- Giphy Capture: Create your gifs from your own videos. https://giphy.com/apps/giphycapture
- Recordit: Screen recording software that allows you to record for tutorials, walk-throughs, video demos and training videos. http://recordit.co
- Vyond: A cloud-based, animated video creation platform with scene and character templates and access to a library of background music. https://www.vyond.com
- Repurpose: A tool to automatically repurpose your audio and video, such as turning a podcast or a Facebook Livestream into a YouTube video. https://repurpose.io

Video editing

- iMovie: Edit video on your smartphone or on desktop. Available free for Mac and iOS on the App Store (and packaged with most Apple products).
- PowerDirector: Edit video on your smartphone or on desktop. Available free on the App Store and Google Play.

Transcription

- Rev: A transcription, caption, subtitling and translation service for all audio and video types. https://www.rev.com
- Otter: A note-taking app that helps you retain, search and share your voice conversations. https://otter.ai

PowerPoint

- Haiku Deck: Presentation software with pre-designed templates. https://www.haikudeck.com

E-book design

- Designrr: Transform your blog posts, podcasts, videos and PDFs into e-books, show notes, dynamic flipbooks, transcripts and blog posts. https://designrr.io
- Printfriendly: This tool cleans and formats web pages for the perfect print experience. https://www.printfriendly.com

Access social media data for your country using these URLs

- https://datareportal.com
- https://napoleoncat.com/stats
- http://gs.statcounter.com/social-media-stats
- https://www.statista.com/topics/1164/social-networks

Index

Find Out More & Connect with Joanne Sweeney

· · · · · · · ·

Learn more at:

publicsectormarketingpros.com

digitaltraininginstitute.ie

Work with Public Sector Marketing Institute and connect with Joanne

Are you a public sector pro?

- Join our global community now and access CPD-accredited live and on-demand social media and digital marketing training

- Benefit from an exclusive discount on all our programmes because you bought this book!

- Go to publicsectormarketingpros.com, choose your course and use the discount code **psmpbook**

🎙 Subscribe to our podcast

Public Sector Marketing Show Podcast is available on all podcast platforms, including Spotify, Google Podcast, iTunes, Stitcher and more.

📡 Subscribe to our blog

publicsectormarketingpros.com/blog

▶ Subscribe to our YouTube Channel

Public Sector Marketing Show

🐦 Twitter

@jstweetsdigital
@publicsectorpro

🔗 Facebook

Joanne Sweeney
Public Sector Marketing Institute

📷 Instagram

@jsgramsdigital
@publicsectormarketingpros

♪ TikTok

@jstiktoks
@socialmediapros

🔗 LinkedIn

Joanne Sweeney
Public Sector Marketing Institute

▶ YouTube

Public Sector Marketing Show

✉ Email

Contact us directly by emailing **info@publicsectormarketingpros.com** and writing '*Public Sector Marketing Pro Book*' in the subject line.

Your Notes

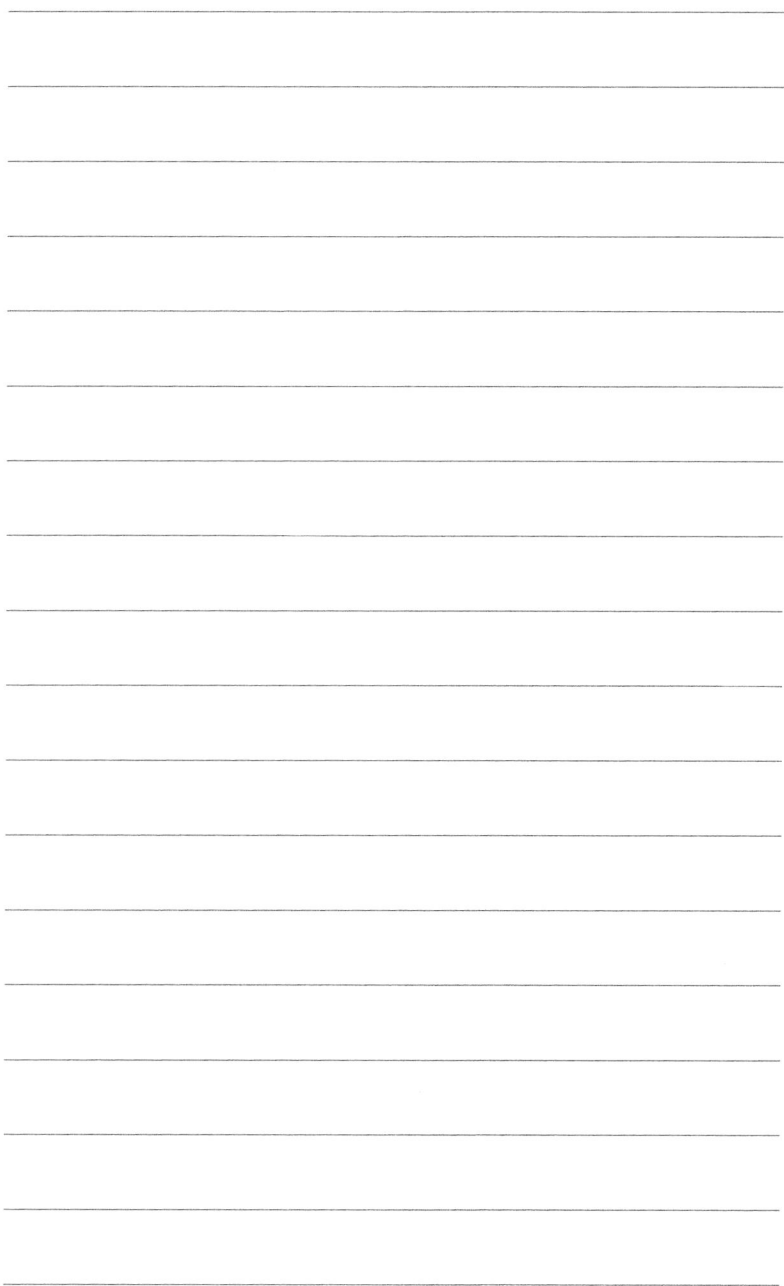

www.ingramcontent.com/pod-product-compliance
Lightning Source LLC
Chambersburg PA
CBHW030456210326
41597CB00013B/693